REBECCA'S JOURNEY

Memoir of a Young Girl Fleeing Antisemitism in Russia

Regina Gershman

Agora Books™
Ottawa, Canada

REBECCA'S JOURNEY: Memoir of a Young Girl Fleeing Antisemitism in Russia

Agora Books
P.O. Box 24191
300 Eagleson Road
Kanata, Ontario K2M 2C3

Agora Books is a self-publishing agency for authors that was launched by The Agora Cosmopolitan which is a registered not-for-profit corporation.

ISBN: 978-1-927538-83-8 (paperback)

Printed in Canada

Contents

INTRODUCTION

OCTOBER 30, 1975.

Rebecca peered out the window of the plane, her mind miles away. With every minute, the plane grew closer to its destination. Rebecca's anticipation grew with the realization that only a couple of hours separated her from the new land – Canada. Though she was scared, she was also excited to start a new life in this new, foreign country. She looked over at her parents and her younger brother, Misha. Mama looked very nervous, while Papa was trying to read a book to ease his anxiety, and Misha was sleeping peacefully.

Rebecca, who grew up in Russia, and was now eleven years old, was glad to finally reach Canada. She knew nothing about it, aside from being able to find it on a map She did know this: Canada and the US were viewed by the Soviet Union as enemies of the state. As a result, even mentioning the names of those two countries were forbidden in Soviet schools, and in Russian society. Reflecting on this, Rebecca smiled at the knowledge that one day her children would be born safely on Canadian soil without any persecution, threats, discrimination, or constant possibility of being exiled without warning. Canada was a free country, with freedom of speech, and freedom to be respected for what one had to say, as opposed to being terrorized by it.

Rebecca's journey was not an easy one for a little girl. She and her parents traveled to not just one country, but three, in less than seven months. People were not always kind to the immigrants, and language was always a barrier. But still fate had brought her and her family to this land full of promise and freedom, to live and exist.

And so my story begins…

Chapter One

An Education

STUDENTS ARE FIRST CALLED *OKTIABRONOK* (also known as "October child") in honour of the October revolution of 1917. As an *Oktiabronok,* I was required to wear a five-pointed red star on the left side of my chest. At age nine, I was called a "Pioneer." When I graduated to Pioneer, a red cotton neckerchief replaced the star. Graduating to Pioneers was a big honour, and it was also a big responsibility, since this was a mandatory duty. As a Pioneer, I spent many hours after school in politically inclined meetings.

I remember sitting next to my friend Alla and listening to our teacher, Mrs. Berdichevsky. We were in a room that was absolutely freezing, so Alla and I sat close together. Alla whispered a joke in my ear about a boy we both liked, and we both burst out laughing. "How dare you interrupt the class? What is so funny Rebecca? Please, tell the class if you think it is so important that you must interrupt me."

Mrs. Berdichevsky was a bitter woman. She hated me because I was Jewish, but she never said that outright. Not yet, at least.

"I'm sorry, Mrs. Berdichevsky," I said. "It will not happen again." Mrs. Berdichevsky bit her cracked, upper lip. Her eyes were full of hatred. I was quite familiar with this hatred. By this time, I was used to it. I prepared myself for a beating, but on this day, I got lucky. "Don't be such an idiot next time," she told me in her annoyingly high, squeaky voice in front of the whole class. "Get away from Alla. Take your seat at the back of the class and shut up."

I took my books and moved to a seat in the back of the room, where it felt even colder without my friend. I was exhausted from a full day at school. I could barely keep my eyes open. I played with my new red neckerchief while the teacher wasn't looking.

In these meetings, we were trained to become more involved, more alert to our surroundings, and more aware of the people around us. Mrs. Berdichevsky began talking about Brezhnev, the leader of the Soviet Union. His name was written on the chalkboard before us. I thought all of this was silly. I thought Mrs. Berdichevsky's blind enthusiasm for this man, the party, and this class, was silly. But I didn't dare say that. Saying anything even remotely critical would result in a beating. Especially if you were Jewish. She began her lecture.

"America bombed the Japanese in World War Two without any reason. Did you know this, children? Do you know that they murdered those people for absolutely no reason? Do you want to know something else about America? People over there do not have jobs. They are lazy, and their government does not care about them. In America, there is a tremendous shortage of jobs, and the women and the children go hungry. *Here*, everyone has a job. Even Jews have a job. Do you know why? Because we look after our people. Brezhnev and the party care about you and they care about me."

Mrs. Berdichevsky began pacing around the room. She held a long ruler in her hand. I too was familiar with this ruler. The marks on my left hand reminded me of the beatings I took when I was younger. Then she pointed to the boy we both liked, Alex. Alex was a handsome boy, and he was also Jewish, but he didn't look as Jewish as I did. He blended in with the other boys, just like my father blended in with the other men. "Alex, why is it important to watch your neighbour?" Mrs. Berdichevsky asked. Alex stuttered a little when he was nervous. "To listen for traitors," said Alex.

"You are half right," said Mrs. Berdichevsky. "Yes, we are looking for traitors, but we also listen to our friends, and our neighbours, so that we can protect our comrades and we can protect the party. Listening to your neighbours is a good deed. It serves the party, and if you serve the party you will live a good life. You will become respectable. You will be an honourable comrade. Remember this and remember it well."

Individuality was strongly frowned upon, and the school taught children of collectivism and nothing else. Everyone was also expected to enrol in *Komsomol* (pre-Communist) party. If a student didn't enrol, other students would ostracize them.

When the class ended, I dreaded the long walk back to my parent's apartment in the cold. I walked part of the way with Alla, and she apologized for getting me in trouble.

Alla's parents cut her hair using a bowl intended for baking cakes. She had a bob cut, and it looked cute, but also quite clumsy.[1]

1. In Russia, back then they didn't have hair salons, so women cut hair for their entire family. Since they didn't have special cutting equipment, they would use hats, or cooking bowls, and place them on the children's heads and cut the hair around.

Alla was not as pretty like I was, and she knew this. I thought she was insecure because she always asked me if she was pretty. I would say yes, but then she would say, "you're just saying that to be nice. You don't really mean it."

As we walked, we had to turn our backs to the wind. The wind was bitter and stung our faces. The neckerchief we were given was made of thin cotton, and did nothing to stop the cold. I was frustrated and overtired.

I took off my neckerchief and threw it in the snow when nobody was watching me. Alla was the only one who saw. "Why would you do that!" Alla was truly shocked.

"I hate Mrs. Berdichevsky, and I have had worse punishments than being called an idiot. She's mild compared to the rest of the teachers," I told Alla.

Despite the wind and the cold, massive lineups of people stood outside. There were lines for meat, dairy and bread. Meat was almost impossible to get, and sometimes one had to wait five hours just to get a decent amount of food for their families.

As I said goodbye to Alla and continued on my way, a disheveled man in a lineup outside a grocery store jumped out at me. He blocked my way. The man had the bulbous nose of an alcoholic, and his angry and bruised visage suggested he had just gotten into a fight. "Give me something to buy a little drink," he told me. "I have no *kopeks*," I told the man. He was very frightening.

Without warning, the man put his disgusting hands on me and shook me to hear if I had any coins in my pocket. "Get out

---

Mothers were always busy and in a rush, and didn't really care how the hair came out to be. There were two types of haircuts allowed in schools. It was pigtails (braided hair), or completely short hair. Long hair was not allowed without be braided. Shoulder length hair was not allowed. It had to be short.

of here," he told me, putting me back down. I ran the rest of the way home. The streets were not safe for little girls. Sadly, such an encounter was not surprising. The country was rife with alcoholism, though alcoholism did not hurt the Jewish people as much as it did for others. An incident like this was unpleasant for me, but by the tender age of nine, I had already grown used to it.

Life in Russia was very harsh. Russia's constitution in 1936 was established on one principle, in the name of Joseph Stalin, which has been quoted in every school book in the Soviet Union: "Everyone must work. Thus he who does not work, will not eat.

As long as one worked well, he or she will be fed, but how bad or well was uncertain. If a person stopped working, he or she would be ostracized from society, as this sort of person was thought to be useless and a burden to the rest.

The pension that my grandmother received was very slight, and unable to carry her for more than a week. Even my grandmother had to continue to force her aging body to keep working, and contribute to the expectation of the society, earning only a couple more *rubles* a month. To Russians, one *ruble* (a Soviet dollar) was very precious. However, money was so lean that even a single *kopek* (a Soviet cent) was as valued as a *ruble*.

On March 8th each year, every work official congratulated female employees by reinforcing women to work hard, in order to be well accepted in society, and to be considered dedicated Soviet citizens.

There was absolutely no difference between men and women when it came to contributing to communist society and productivity. Everyone was encouraged to work hard, and produce for the Communist Party.

On days like that organized celebration, participation was mandatory. The names of those in attendance were carefully checked and scrutinized. Those that didn't attend would be reprimanded, punished, and fired.

Not long after Stalin's motto, the names of the days of the week were changed. The Soviet rulers outlawed a 1,000-year-old Russian word, replacing *Voskrisenya* (Sunday) with *wihodnoy* (day off) or more exactly, "the day of outing."

ENGLISH	RUSSIAN	MEANING
Monday	Ponedelnik	The beginning of the week
Tuesday	Vtornik	Second day
Wednesday	Sreda	Middle of the week
Thursday	Chetwerg	Fourth day
Friday	Piatnitza	Fifth day
Saturday	Subbotha	Hebrew "Sabbath"
Sunday	Wihodnoy	Day Off / The Day of Outing

Finally, I reached the local bazaar right next to my first childhood home. There were a few merchants there who I knew. By the age of seven I began doing the shopping for the family, because they would not serve my mother. She looked too stereotypically Jewish. Our first apartment was right next to the bazaar.

Apartments in Kiev were scarce. A person could only get one if they knew someone in the government, or if they paid out money "under the table." The more one paid out, the better place one would receive.

The living arrangements in Kiev were horrendous too. When I was five, my family had to share their living quarters with four other families. There was a communal washroom, which included a tiny toilet and a small, barrel-like, ever-filthy tub. The"kitchen" was a tiny, square cubicle with a sink, and a four-burner stove for five families. Everyone had his or her own assigned bathroom hours and kitchen privileges. Hot water was always a problem.

When one of the families finally moved out, my grandmother moved in with her new husband. Her previous husband, Dmitry, had been killed in the Second World War.

Even with its cramped quarters, a one-room apartment with electricity and running water was considered quite roomy by Russian standards: fifteen feet by fifteen feet, with a window facing the local bazaar. Mama and Papa occupied the largest part of the room. I was off in one corner, and my brother Misha in another. A sofa-bed, (unclear) and a dining table doubled as a drafting table. My father was a drafting engineer, so his table stood in the center.

Nothing else could fit in. There were no closets, so we had to leave our clothing where we could find space, behind the doors on hooks, and make storage spaces on the walls.

It was not long before we managed to get another apartment in a very good location. It even had a dairy store on the ground level, and was right across from the park. Best of all, there were only four of us living there. So, we didn't have to share the kitchen and bathroom with anyone else. What a wonderful treat!

When I arrived home my mother told me to close the curtains. It was *Shabbat*, and we were getting ready for *Shabbat* dinner. My father's grandparents were quite religious. He was a rabbi, and they usually enjoyed hosting us for *Shabbat* dinner, but it had increasingly become more dangerous for us. We decided to start hosting *Shabbat* at my parent's place.

As I helped prepare, I wondered how many Jews would report other Jews to the KGB. I wondered how bad the punishments actually were. Mama handed me the Kiddush cup made from sterling silver. It was such a treat to hold the cold metal in my hands. I loved preparing for the Sabbath. It was such a joyous occasion. However, as I grew older, I became increasingly frustrated that we had to hide our way of life.

My grandfather sat with my father. They spoke with hushed voices and smoked cigarettes before the meal. I helped Mama warm the chicken soup that she had made the night before. The soup was made from frail bones rather than meat, because meat was so difficult to acquire, especially for Jews.

The table was set just as Aunt Polina arrived. Aunt Polina was a jokester, and I enjoyed it when she was able to make it to dinner. The concept of fashion was completely alien to us then. Nobody was "fashionable," but Aunt Polina seemed to have a particular style. It was not so much what she wore, but how she carried herself. She was confident and funny. We said the prayer for the bread and the wine, and I sat next to my Aunt Polina.

We sat in darkness. How I wished we could open the curtains to get light and air.

"How was school?" She asked me. I told Aunt Polina about what we learned, but none of the other unfortunate events I experienced that day. It was tough; you had to be tough to survive such a place. Then I thought it would be okay if I asked Aunt Polina a question that had been on my mind for quite some time.

"Aunt Polina, what happens if we just open the curtains? I'm tired of hiding. People already know we are Jewish. They might as well see how we live. Maybe then they will stop being so mean to us."

Aunt Polina became somber. She sighed and she coughed as though she was deflating. She normally made jokes about everything, but I could tell she was serious when she told me, "Rebecca, I know. But if one neighbour reports us, there is a risk we could be separated. I have already seen…." I saw my mother motioning with her hands to Aunt Polina to stop talking.

"Never mind, sweetheart," said Aunt Polina. "Eat your soup. Enjoy. Let's talk about happy things. I am happy you are doing well at school and that you are friends with that girl. What is her name? Oh yes, Alla. It's good she is not Jewish. It is always good to have a friend who is not Jewish, but be careful. Don't tell her too much. Don't tell her anything that might get you in trouble."

I thought this was a terrible thing to say. But I wondered if it was a mistake to tell Alla about my feelings for Mrs. Berdichevsky. She also knew that I threw my neckerchief away in a fit of rage. Perhaps now, I thought, I would be more careful around Alla.

My father and my grandfather continued to talk after dinner. My father was normally clean-shaven, but he had let a little stubble grow. He was stressed about money. They sat in front of the radio we had, listening to All Union Radio. All of the news was the same. There were no dissenting views or opinions. There were only three channels on the radio and all of the channels broadcasted the voice of Brezhnev.

My father stroked the stubble of his face and spoke with his hands to my grandfather. "There is no question that I need another job. The salary I make is not enough with Rebecca growing older. Her sister, and now her brother. I need to feed my children. The problem is with my propiska (passport)." Everyone was required to carry identification. The third line would state if you are Jewish or not. Despite being skilled as a draftsman, my father could not find work anywhere else. He needed a second job to support the family.

I helped Mama put the food away and got into bed next to my older sister, Lena.

Lena and I shared the same beautiful hair, and she loved to play the piano. After a child completes the tenth grade, the KGB tells you what kind of occupation you are going to have. She began her education at the Royal Conservatory of Music and wanted to go to university to continue to take piano. The communists told her she couldn't because she was Jewish. It was a tragedy. A true tragedy.

Despite being exhausted, I listened intently to my grandfather and father speaking softly. They turned the volume up to All Union Radio, but I could still hear them. The space in the apartment was very intimate. "I think I might have a solution," said my grandfather. "There is no question we must bribe Valarie. The question is how much he will take. If you can work there, you may be able to take some extra cabbage too."

I knew exactly who Valarie was, and where he worked. He worked in a grocery store in the bazaar by our first apartment. He was one of the "friendlier" ones. I decided that I would have to come up with a plan to convince him to hire my Papa.

At the age of seven, I began grocery shopping for the family because Mama was often discriminated against. Being a noticeable Jew, Mama's life was not a happy one. She was constantly persecuted by anti-Semitic remarks from our neighbours and her colleagues at work.

Something as simple as buying groceries was not simple. Often, it became an impossible task, as mean and ill-spirited people would refuse to sell her anything at all. The darkness of civil bigotry was everywhere. Even my own name, Rebecca, was a potential threat to my family and me. Most of the people around us persecuted and looked down upon anyone with a Jewish background. For our family's safety, I was sometimes given a different name to be spoken in public: Regina. I did have one other name, one that I adored: the nickname given to me by Papa. It still warms me to think back to him cheerfully calling me "his little Regoletta."

However, outside our home, the brazen disgust shown to my family continued, regardless of the precautionary steps we took. In one instance, soon after my brother Misha was born, my mother and I went to the bazaar to buy a pitcher of milk. When a saleswoman saw my mother, she purposely closed the door on Mama and cried "next!" How Mama suffered. People walking all over her, and she could do nothing about it. Such a hateful way that people treated her… nobody should have been treated like that.

There were, however, the merchants who took pity on us.

Before sunrise the next day, I woke up and carefully completed all of my morning chores for Mama. I made sure to make as little noise as possible. My task was to buy cabbage for the family after school. Mama awoke as I was getting ready to leave and asked me where I was going. "I'm going to school, Mama," I told her. "So early?"

"Yes, Mama, I want to study before the teacher comes."

It was snowing outside, and the snow was densely packed. It had snowed all night and it was about up to my knees. I trudged through the freshly packed snow until I arrived at the grocery store. Valarie was unloading a truckload of produce. He was a short balding man, and his disposition was very friendly. Outside the store there was a "help wanted" sign, and I knew I was at the right place. "Yes, little girl," he said to me. "You should not be here. Please, we open in an hour."

I waited politely, and when he realized I was not leaving, he shrugged at me. "Okay why aren't you going?" He asked me. "My father needs a job, but he is Jewish," I told Valarie. Valarie frowned at me. I handed him all of the *kopeks* my mother gave me to buy the cabbage, and explained that they were for him. I also explained that my father and grandfather were going to give him more money, so that he could secure the job. "Such a good daughter you are," said Valarie. "Thank you for this," he said.

I had a good feeling when I bribed Valarie. I felt as though he was a man of his word. My innocence was taken away from me at such a young age. It was truly an education to see how the world really worked. I developed a certain kind of intelligence that I believe is more valuable than book smarts. I learned how things actually worked on the streets, and how people actually felt.

My problem now was how to explain to Mama that I had no cabbage to make for soup. Then the solution came to my mind immediately. I would simply take my lunch home for the family. Our schools fed us lunch. The problem was that the Jewish children got all of the leftover and rotten food. I prayed to G-d that the food I would receive that day would be somewhat edible.

I walked to school in the dark. To my astonishment, I found the red neckerchief I had thrown in the snow the day before. I couldn't believe my luck. In the washroom before class begun, I tied it around my neck and checked my hair in the mirror. I made sure my braids were properly tied so that they would not come loose.

All the girls were supposed to wear their hair in double braids, and wear a school uniform. In the hallway, I ran into Alla and asked her to please keep what I had said between us. She promised not to say anything, and we walked together to Mr. Kulic's class.

Mr. Kulic was our mathematics teacher. He was about thirty years old, and intimidating. He had platinum blonde hair and striking green eyes. Many of the girls had crushes on him, but

I thought he was brutish. I was fortunate enough to be good at math. He never really paid much attention to me, and I was fine with that. When lunch time came, I said goodbye to Alla. All of the Jewish, black, Asian and Tatar children sat together. If Alla was seen with me in the cafeteria, I would get in trouble. We were separated in the cafeteria, but not in class, because we were not allowed to eat the same food.

The food Alla was given was fresh and nutritious, but the other children were given old *borsht* or soups or salads, that were two, or sometimes three days old. Our cafeteria lady, Tatiana, served us our meals. She was a stout woman who wore too much makeup and smelled like onions. I saw Alla from across the cafeteria and waved to her. How I wish I could just sit with my friend.

The good news was that Alex was sitting next to me. I talked with Alex. "The teachers seem to like you," I told Alex. "I don't think they do," he said. "I think they just tolerate me." I told Alex not to speak that way, and that many people liked him. He looked up at me. "They do?" "Yes," I told him. "I like you."

Alex blushed. He was not sure what to say, and I was shocked that I said it in the way that I did. Tatiana came over and gave us both a serving of tomato *borsht* and salad. It was horrible, and I did not want to eat it, but I had no choice. I started with the salad because I wanted to get it over with. The leaves were brown with spots of little black mold. I ate two or three bites, but it was repugnant. I started throwing up at the table, and Tatiana immediately saw this and ran out from the kitchen.

"What is wrong with you Rebecca? What kind of mess have you made!" She yelled at me. I tried to say sorry, but I threw up again. There was vomit all over the table and my cafeteria tray. Alex covered his mouth. I thought he was going to start throwing up too. Lena produced a spoon from her apron and scooped up the vomit and put it on my tray.

"Eat it. You will not waste food in my cafeteria," she shouted. I shoved more food from my tray into my mouth with the vomit and then vomited again. All of the children began to laugh and Alex began to cry. I told him it would be okay, but Lena grabbed me by the ear and walked me to principal Boyko's office to explain my behaviour.

My school uniform was stained, and I had tears running down my face. The principal's office was a foreboding place. There were two wicker chairs set up outside his office, and I hated the feeling of sitting on those chairs. I could not look the principal Boyko directly in the eye. In fact, I was instructed not to. He was so skinny and tall that I would have had to tilt my little head upwards to do this. I was looking at his polished brown shoes.

"Lena tells me that you were ungrateful for your food. Why were you ungrateful?" "I don't know sir," I said. Principal Boyko shook his head. "That is not an acceptable answer, Rebecca. You need to learn the importance of gratitude." Principal Boyko buzzed his secretary to call my mathematics teacher, Mr. Kulic. "I am too old to properly discipline you, Rebecca," said principal Boyko. "Perhaps Mr. Kulic can persuade you. Wait for him outside."

I sat on the wicker chair waiting for Mr. Kulic to come. I remember this was the first time I did not feel paralyzed with fear. The fear was certainly there. I knew the beating was coming. What I was surprised with, was the anger that was boiling in my breast. This anger was against the injustice. "It is so unjust," I told myself over and over again. "I do not deserve this."

Mr. Kulic arrived and led me to a small, stuffy room with shaggy carpeting and no windows. There was a small desk and a chair by the door to the room. I sat in the chair while Mr. Kulic sat at the desk and wrote down a disciplinary report. "You know what you did wrong, isn't that right Rebecca?" He asked me. "Yes," I said. "Close the door," he grunted. Mr. Kulic told me to stand up and face the wall. He took off his belt and whipped my bottom extraordinarily hard. I was winded by how hard the first blow was, and I could feel my flesh sting beneath my dress.

"Owwwww!" I screamed. "Shut up!" He yelled at me. I grinded my teeth together as he whipped me another ten times and I did not scream at all. Blood dripped down my leg and stained my socks. "Alright, turn around. I've given you enough for today." When I turned around, Mr. Kulic was grinning, and I could see the horrible gap in between his teeth. "You have such a pretty smile," he told me. "You are lucky there are other girls here that are prettier than you." I did not know what that meant at the time, and it chills me to this day. I never found out if he assaulted any of the other girls.

In the washroom, I checked to see the damage. He had broken the skin even though he whipped me with my dress on. I had never been whipped so hard before. I cleaned the blood and lightly touched my bruises. Sitting down would be difficult for the next week.

Later I saw Alex and he asked me if I was okay. I told him that I was, and we walked out together. I loved the end of the day. I loved the short moment of freedom I felt. Then it occurred to me that I still needed to buy cabbage for Mama, and that I had no *kopeks* because I had given it all to Valarie. I told Alex about it.

"Ta…ta…ta…take some of my *kopeks* and buy what you need," he told me. "You are so sweet," I said. Then Alex kissed me on the cheek. I was not expecting that at all, and I turned bright red. "I like you too," said Alex. "See you tomorrow." Alex walked away and I felt on top of the world. I could not wait to tell Alla about what happened, but then I wondered if I should. I began my walk to the grocery store, but my mind was in the clouds. I could not stop thinking about Alex.

I decided to go back to Valarie to buy the cabbage, and as I stood in line, I was smiling from ear to ear. "What are you so happy about?" an old woman grunted at me in line. "I'm just happy," I told her. She shook her head. "Well stop it. It's annoying," she told me.

When I saw Valarie again, I asked him if he was going to hire my father. "Yes. The money you gave me is a good start. If he can give me a couple more *rubles*, that would be good too. Tell him that if he can't, he can start immediately. I will just deduct what he owes me from his pay." I thanked Valarie multiple times for his "kindness" and walked to buy some other essentials for Mama.

Regardless of whether you were Jewish or not, it was never easy to buy something in a Soviet store. If you wished to buy some cheese, you would go to the cheese counter. But instead of receiving the product, you would be given a ticket. "Take it over there, child!" the saleswoman pointed to the corner where a cashier sat. "Go pay at the cashier over there. Come back to the counter, there. See?" and she pointed to another clerk. "That girl will give you the cottage cheese." The procedure in all the stores of the Soviet Union was devised by the government in such a manner that a shopper had to stand not only once in line, and not twice, but three times in order to collect the purchased item.

People ran toward the stores, especially people who were on their way home from work, because they knew they'd be stranded there for at least two hours. The prices were not the same for everybody either. If you were a communist, the price was set lower then if you were a non-party member.

Tania, a college graduate, started working, and was receiving a salary three times as much as my mother, only because she was married to a communist, while Mama already had fifteen years of experience on the job. But it didn't matter.

The line-ups in the stores were often brutal, especially on Sundays. Sunday was the only day when Russians could truly relax, as they only had a one-day holiday each week.

A typical Soviet Sunday at the store included people in lines jumping, and yelling, and their children crying.

My little brother Misha was playing, and my sister was studying a Mazurka No. 10 in B-Flat Major, Op. 17, No.1 by Chopin. She was playing the piece in the air with her long, nimble fingers. She was imagining the keys, and I thought that when I got a little older, I wanted to be just like her. We even looked the same. I had the same fingers, but we had no piano to practice on. Instead my sister took lessons. I dreamed of the day when I would ask Mama for piano lessons.

"Do me a favour and feed Misha," my exhausted Mama told me. I put the groceries by the stove and Mama looked relieved to see them. "Good. You have gotten everything. I am so sorry you had to wait in line for some measly cabbage. I wish I could have gone myself to get it. How was school?" Whenever Mama asked me how school was, I would always say it was fine. She had too much to worry about. I gave Misha some milk and little pieces of bread to munch on. I loved taking care of Misha. It felt so good to see the smile on his face.

My father was sitting in front of the radio looking over his drawings. I was always amazed at how complex and detailed the drawings were. The lines were absolutely perfect because Papa used special tools and had a very steady hand. "I went to Valarie and gave him a few *kopeks* so that you can get the job, Papa," I told him. "Why would you do that!" He raised his voice at me. "I'm sorry, I thought I was helping you," I said, about to cry. Papa picked me up and kissed me on the forehead. "I love you, but sometimes you are too curious for your own good. Please, you must ask me about such things."

The day I had was too much for me to handle, and I began to cry. Papa consoled me and Mama asked him what was wrong. "She was fine when she came in, now she's crying? I don't understand why." When I calmed down, I told Papa what Valarie said, and he told me to promise not to involve myself again with such matters. I promised him that I would not. "I know you care, my little Regoletta, but Valarie could have easily reported us for what you did. We have to be sure he is not going to say anything to the KGB. It not only impacts me. It could have hurt the whole family."

I felt terrible for what I did, and that night I could not sleep. I was laying on my side because of the bruises on my behind. Thankfully I did have one fond thought. Alex. He was such a kind boy. It was not a sexual thing at that age. We just felt an affinity for one another. We were becoming close, Alex and me.

There was a feeling I had when I woke up in the morning, on most days, that I did not want to go to school. It was a feeling of dread more than fear. It was a feeling of being trapped. The teachers did not understand me, and I did not understand them. How could they be so cruel toward the Jews? What was the reason for this?

I walked to school with my sister Lena, and I saw that she had a book in her satchel that was different than the rest. When she saw that I spotted it, she quickly tried to hide it. "What book is that?" I asked. Lena sighed. "Ah, you should not have seen that Rebecca. You are too aware." I thought this was a strange comment to make. "What does that mean, too aware? Is it better to be dull? I want to know."

Lena looked around to make sure nobody was listening. "It's some notes I have about Aleksandr Solzhenitsyn. The notes are about a book he wrote called One Day in the Life of Ivan Denisovich. Don't mention his name at all. Don't talk to anybody about it."

"Why?" I asked.

"Because you will be punished if you do, and you will put the family at risk," my sister told me. "Then why are you reading it if it's so risky?" I asked Lena. "Just focus on going to school and doing what the teacher tells you to. Don't be such a troublemaker," Lena told me.

I loved my sister, but she didn't understand me. Things came easier for her, but we loved each other. She would do anything for me. She was telling me these things to make my life a little easier, but I would have none of it. Even at this young age I felt I was different than the other children. I was a rebel and I always longed for justice. I hated this palpable feeling of not belonging. It was suffocating to feel this way. What I hated more was that there was no reason I could find to justify it. I did not know why I was so different, and I wanted to know why.

My sister left me, and I met up with Alla before Mrs. Berdichevsky's class. I could tell immediately that something was wrong with Alla. Her voice was cold, and she was not friendly towards me at all. "What's the matter?" I asked her. "You know what's the matter," she sneered. "No," I said. "I don't know. Why are you mad?"

Alla huffed and gave me a little shove. "You know. Alex. Alex likes you."

"How do you know?" I asked her.

"I saw him kiss you on the cheek," she told me. "You're a lying Jew. And I'm telling Mrs. Berdichevsky about what you did to your neckerchief. I'm telling her that you threw it in the snow and that you told me you hate her. Watch me do it after class," she whispered in my ear.

We took our seats. This time I went to the back of the class voluntarily. I did not want to sit next to Alla after what she told me. I also knew I couldn't change her mind. Mrs. Berdichevsky was talking again about Brezhnev, but I could not focus. We had to write something down and I began writing with my left hand because I was so distraught.

When I was learning how to write, I naturally wrote with my left hand, but the teachers beat my left hand with a ruler so hard until it bled so that I could not use the hand to write or eat. The scars and the memories were still fresh, but my mind was so preoccupied with Alla that I did not realize I was writing with my left hand again.

Mrs. Berdichevsky immediately noticed that I was not writing with my correct hand and yelled at me. "Idiot! Are you a baby? How have you forgotten how to write? Write with your proper hand, Rebecca."

I quickly switched hands but Alla called Mrs. Berdichevsky over, and the two of them spoke out of earshot. I knew what they were talking about, because Mrs. Berdichevsky was looking at me with growing fire in her eyes. She strutted over and ripped the pen out of my hand. The ink from the pen dripped all over my paper. Russian and Ukrainian schools did not use the types of pens and pencils that we see today. Instead, they were pens that needed to be filled up with ink all the time. A small ink container could always be seen on pupils' desks.

"Look what you did," she told me. "Look at how clumsy you are. Alla tells me you don't like me very much. Is this true?" she asked me. "No," I said. I was shaking. "Well, I guess it's true what they say about the Jews being sneaky liars. Alla tells me you said you hated me, and that you tossed your neckerchief in the snow."

"It's not true!" I yelled.

"Shut up! I have had enough of this. Stand up," Mrs. Berdichevsky shouted at me. She grabbed me by my neckerchief and escorted me outside the school. We were standing outside, in the snow. "Extend your left hand out," she commanded. I put my left hand out and she beat it with her ruler, like the teachers before her. She kept smacking my knuckles until the skin broke. Blood streamed down my hand and dripped into the snow. Then I heard a loud crack and I felt an excruciating pain electrify my index and middle finger. I thought they might have broken.

"Good. Now go see principal Boyko." I went to the principal's office and sat on the wicker chair again. The distain inside me only grew with each visit. Principal Boyko leaned back in his chair and shook his head of silver hair like he did before. "It seems like you are not learning, Rebecca. Well, if the belt doesn't work once. I say, try it again until it does. Wait for Mr. Kulic outside. I would do it myself, but I am too old and weak to discipline you."

I found myself in the small room again with Mr. Kulic. The scabs from the last beating were still fresh, but this time he struck me even harder, if that was even possible. "I'm getting tired of doing this. You better not find yourself alone with me again, Rebecca," he told me.

Alex was outside and I waved to him, but he was apprehensive as he came over to me. "That looks so bad, does it hurt really bad?" he asked me. "No, it's fine," I said. I was trying to act cool.

My hand had begun swelling up. It was red and puffy, and I could not walk properly from the second beating I received from Mr. Kulic. "Do you want to walk me home?" I asked Alex. "I want to, but I don't want the other kids to see. I'm sorry," he told me.

I felt devastated that Alex said that. I thought he was strong like I was, but I was wrong. I didn't feel like talking to him after that. Now I had no friends, and as I walked home I thought about this and cried to myself. The drunks on the street were everywhere, and I ducked into alleyways to avoid them. I did not want to go home, so I roamed around the streets for a while, aimlessly.

I sat watching the line-ups of people. I enjoyed listening to their conversations and hearing what the adults had to say. The bazaar by my old apartment was an interesting place to sit and observe. Two women were having a lively conversation, and so I listened in. One of the ladies was named Dina, and she was talking with her friend Olga. Dina had just come back from Moscow.

"When I was in Moscow, I saw a lineup of people, and I naturally got in line. I did not even think about what the line was for. Then I realized that this line up was for bananas. I had never tasted bananas. So, after two and a half hours, I come to the front of the line and the grocer says, 'oh, sorry no more bananas.' I was crushed, but then a man took pity on me and tossed me one of his, and I could not believe how good this banana was. It was sweet and ripe. I cried when I ate this banana. I was in the middle of Moscow, crying."

"That's quite a story," said Olga.

When I arrived home, I asked Mama if she thought we would ever be able to buy bananas. "Where do you get these ideas from," she asked me. "I don't know," I said. As I was helping her prepare dinner, she noticed my hands and dropped the ladle for the soup. "My G-d, how did this happen?" she asked me. "My teacher did it to me," I told her. I broke down crying. I could not take the pain of that day, and Mama stroked my head. She consoled me in a way only a mother could.

"This is unsustainable. We will leave Kiev," she told me softly, so that nobody else could hear. "Something needs to change. We can't keep living like this." Mama did not yet know how, but she was intent on leaving Kiev as soon as possible, and making a better life for her family in a free country. It was, of course, not that easy back then.

My father walked in with a big smile on his face. This made us all smile. "What is it?" asked Mama. "I got a second job. Valarie hired me, and now I have two days more of work."

"That's wonderful," said Mama. "Congratulations," my sister Lena exclaimed. She gave him a big hug.

I made sure to hide my hand in my dress so that nobody else would see. I also forced myself to walk without limping despite the pain underneath my dress. When I slept at night, I could only sleep on my right side. I listened to the radio along with my father. The days of winter felt so long and dark. I longed for the spring.

Despite everything that I had gone through in school, my suffering was only beginning. I could not sit idly by while everyone walked all over me. I thought I had to fight back in some way. Besides, I thought, I had nothing to lose because I was already being beaten and ridiculed, even if I complied or showed remorse for my alleged "misbehaviour."

I was in Mr. Kulic's mathematics class one day when a mischievous boy named Bogdan was bullying me. The seating plan was boy, girl, boy, girl and so on. He was seated behind me and he kept whispering terrible insults. "Why are you such a dirty Jew?" he asked me. I did not even bother to respond. I turned around and made a face at him. Later on in the lesson he grabbed one of my braids and dipped the end of it in his ink well. The whole class, including Mr. Kulic, started to laugh as I burst into tears. It was far more than "boys being boys."

Chapter Two

Fighting Back

I had finally had enough. My heart was filled with rage. I wanted Bogdan to get what he deserved. On the playground, I found Bogdan and I went right up to his face. "Look at my hair. Do you think it's funny what you did? Do you enjoy tormenting me the way you do?" Bogdan laughed at me.

He laughed in my face with his little rat-like teeth. He wore thick rimmed glasses, so I grabbed them off his face and shoved him. Bogdan fell backwards and then tumbled awkwardly onto his side. He screamed in pain. "My arm, my arm. You broke it!"

"No, I didn't, you baby. How could a girl break your arm?"

I did not break his arm, but I did dislocate it. He screamed in pain and the children around me looked at me with shock. They backed away from me. I knew I was going to be given the belt again, but I felt good. I felt justice was finally served. I found myself in the principal's office. Mr. Kulic told Principal Boyko that he did not think he could hit me any harder than he did before.

"If I hit her any harder, she won't be able to walk home," said Mr. Kulic. Principal Boyko was sipping hot tea. The steam fogged up his wire rimmed glasses. He looked down upon me with hatred. It was as if I was subhuman. "Good, then let her crawl home in the snow."

"Maybe then she will learn not to behave like such an animal."

He took a closer look at me. For the first time, he looked deeply into my eyes. "Rebecca, that poor boy is going to suffer in a cast because of you. You sent him to the hospital, and now I have to explain to his parents that a little Jewish girl did this to him. Do you understand how humiliating that is? Do you understand that your actions have consequences?" His condescending tone drove me mad. I wanted to shout at him, but I was satisfied with what I had done to that little boy. He deserved exactly what he got.

I did not answer the principal. I took my beating in the small room I had grown so familiar with. Mr Kulic, for the first time ever, did not display as much joy in beating me. At first, I thought perhaps there was a chance he had a conscience. Unsurprisingly, this was not the case. He was simply melancholic. He whipped me, but it felt lighter than before. "At first I enjoyed beating you. Now I'm just sick at the sight of you. Why can't you just do as your told? Why do you people have to be a constant plague we must deal with?" Mr. Kulic asked these questions out loud, and I wanted to answer him. I wanted to shout at the top of my lungs that he was the real monster in this room.

After the beating, it truly was difficult to walk. I sat in the snow for a while after school. I did not have the strength to move. The school year was not even close to ending, but it felt like the longest year of my life. I wanted new teachers, a new school and new friends. I desperately needed new friends I felt so isolated and alone. I needed my sister. I needed to talk to her and tell her more about what was happening with me.

When I got home, she was again studying music, and I asked her if she could teach me anything. She seemed irritated, but she reluctantly agreed and taught me a basic scale. "I want to learn how to play the piano like you do. I wish we had a piano at home to practice on," I said.

"Maybe when you are a little older you can ask Mama to take you for lessons," said Lena. My sister was so graceful and humble. She was so smart too. I asked her about her secret book, and if I could read it. "What did I say about talking about the book! Don't mention it again. I'll give it to you when you're older and you can understand." I was always deeply interested in learning, and I learned from a young age that when my teachers or other adults would become mad, I was onto something. The first time I learned about the dissident movement was when I spotted my sister's book. I did not know the historical significance of visionaries like Aleksandr Solzhenitsyn or Andrei Sakharov. In the west, they were renowned thinkers, but we were living in a bubble. The Soviet regime had sentenced those with a dissenting opinion to mental hospitals.

The radio and the television had three channels, and when Brezhnev gave a speech, he was on all three. There was never another opinion.

I was ten years old in 1974. I was still bullied because of being Jewish, and the students were still cruel. At that time, I became fascinated with the subject of psychiatry.

In my school's library, I began spending my time reading about Sigmund Freud. This was a very rare thing to do for a child as young as ten. For me it was an easy task. The homework was easy, and I could complete it quickly. I wanted to read books that piqued my interest, so I would hide books I read about Sigmund Freud inside my schoolwork. Nobody bothered me.

After some time, Alex felt it was safe to associate with me again, and so we began eating lunch together again in the cafeteria. I pretended to eat the food to appease the teachers, but in reality, I just shovelled the food into my satchel without them seeing. As a result, I lost a lot of weight. Alex was sorry that he had "abandoned" me, but I told him it was all right. I told him that we had to stick together.

I asked him if he thought I was crazy. "I don't think you are crazy," said Alex. He was munching on his salad and I could not believe he was able to stomach it. "My aunt from New York is coming to stay with us," he told me one day. "I can't believe it," I said. "Are you lying?"

"No. I'm serious," said Alex.

We began walking home together again and a few days later, I saw his aunt. She had unusual clothing to our Soviet eyes: bell bottom jeans and a colourful sweater. American clothing looked superb. She also looked healthy and fit. Alex introduced us.

"This is my Aunt Yana," said Alex. Yana was very tall, and had blonde hair, immaculately straight and smooth. I told her that she had very beautiful hair. The bellbottom jeans fit her body well, compared to the jeans I saw on the street. Blue jeans were just becoming legalized, and bought on the black market, but they looked nothing like the real thing from America.

"Why thank you, darling. What a wonderful compliment. You are such a polite young lady."

I wanted to ask her about the Japanese. "Is it true about how the Americans bombed the Japanese for no reason?" Yana looked uncomfortable. "Well they did bomb the Japanese, but that was because they were fighting with the Nazis."

This confused me. I wanted to ask more questions, but they had to go.

I had more questions for Alex, and the next time we spoke in the cafeteria. "I don't think we should talk about it here, Rebecca. The teachers are listening to us," he told me. Alex was right. It was risky to speak this openly, so I insisted that I walk to school with Alex every day.

In the morning I would wake up, do my chores with Mama, help feed my baby brother and say goodbye to Papa and Lena. Then I would walk two blocks away to Alex's house. His stutter seemed to be getting better. He was less nervous around me. We were becoming good friends now.

"Please tell me more about Yana. I am very interested to know what she knows, about America." Alex always looked both ways before telling me anything. It was silly sometimes because we could both tell nobody was listening. Still, Alex was very cautious. "Yana was telling our family that we should move to Israel. She came to tell us about our family there, and about how different life is." It was astonishing to hear my friend Alex speak this way. I thought I needed to learn more about Israel, and I needed to tell Papa. Papa was working for Valerie two nights a week now.

When he came home, he smelled like the market. There was a particular smell to Valarie's store. Underneath his apron he produced two heads of cabbage. He took some cabbage here and there, so that we could survive. Otherwise there was not enough food for us.

One evening he came home, exhausted. He needed to rest, but he still had drawings to do. After dinner was finished, he told Mama and me to forget about cleaning up. "Let's go out for a walk. Let's enjoy this marvellous spring weather," he told me.

We took a stroll up and down the street, and he asked me about school. I told him about my friend Alex and about Israel. I asked Papa if he could look into moving there. "I am already looking into this my little Regoletta. I am speaking to my friends, and I am seeing what can be done."

I was so happy to hear Papa say this, and I wanted to know more about Israel and more about when we could move there. The Soviet Union had lifted its ban on the Jewish Refusenik, which was the ban to emigrate to Israel, in 1971. Now it was a few years afterward, and Alex's story was the first I had heard of such an adventure.

We returned from our walk and we were standing outside our building, taking in the lovely air of spring. It was so wonderful to hear the birds chirping and feel the sun on my skin. Mama closed her eyes and smiled for the first time in what felt like months.

Two men approached us. They were young hoodlums, and they had vodka in their hands. "Is that your wife?" asked one of the men quite rudely. "Yes, what business of it is yours?" The other hoodlum grinned. "She looks like a Jew. And you are married to her?" Papa slowly stepped forward, so that Mama and I were behind him. "Yes, what business of it of yours?" Mama begged Papa to leave, but he stood his ground. We watched in terror. We did not want them to hurt Papa, but these men were young and strong. They were both clearly drunk.

"So, you work at the market, eh? How does a Jew get a job at the market, while I'm stuck shovelling garbage all day? I'll tell you how, because the Jews run the world. Those American Jews have all the money. They run the world. That's how." Papa slowly backed up and the hoodlums lost focus. They were too drunk to fight. We retreated into the apartment and slammed the door behind us.

This was a rare event where Papa experienced antisemitism. The lack of venom spewed at him was based on how he didn't "look" like a Jew. As a result, Papa never had to bear the antisemitism shown his wife.

Then a few weeks after our unpleasant encounter, something exciting happened. Papa returned home with a new radio, capable of listening to signals far away. At night, he would turn on the radio and we could listen to Kol Ha Shalom, otherwise known as the Voice of Peace. We would also listen to the BBC.

Papa told us we had to be careful, because if anybody found out and reported us to the KGB, we would be severely punished. It was strange to listen to Hebrew and to English spoken in such a strange way. I heard about disco for the first time, listening to the radio.

I told Alex the next day at school that we had gotten a new radio and that we could listen to what was happening in Israel. The Jewish people who wanted to emigrate from the Soviet Union were amongst the most successful people who rebelled. I would learn this many years later. Brave men and women from the United States like Alex's aunt Yana were critical in helping Soviet Jews.

Alex told me that his family was planning on moving to Tel Aviv, but that it would be some time before they had enough money saved to do so.

Once, when we were leaving school, we saw an elderly man in a fight with a militia member. During these years, certain words became outlawed, and the government decided to change them. The common word for "officer" became "commander", "police" was now "militia", and "Mr./Mrs." became "citizen/comrade."

The man was shouting at the young "militia" member. He was drunk and complaining that he had not been able to eat a decent meal in years. "You stupid child!" he shouted. "You don't know what real food even tastes like! This is no way to live. I would rather die than live here, with you, baby comrade."

The militia member blew his whistle and they apprehended the man. "That's enough out of you," he shouted. "We are taking you to where you belong."

"Oh yeah? Where do I belong comrade?"

"The mental hospital," he said. "Good," shouted the old man. "Take me away. Call me crazy, but know that I'm not. You are the crazy one, comrade! You can rot in hell," he yelled.

The Brezhnev-era Soviet regime became famous for sending anybody who rebelled against them to mental hospitals. Anyone who complained about the bread lines or how little money they had were labeled by the KGB as "crazy" and sent to these places. The radio openly reported such events to scare us, and I wanted to see one of these facilities for myself.

I once asked Alex if he was interested in visiting a mental hospital with me, and he declined. I suppose seeing the old man being taken away changed Alex's mind. He asked if he could come with, and we traveled to one of these hospitals located near St. Sophia's Cathedral. The walls were tall and made from grey concrete. Guards stood outside the hospital. It looked more like prison than a hospital.

We sat on a bench opposite the hospital and watched it for a while. "Maybe we should go," said Alex.

"I don't like how afraid you are all the time. Stop being so afraid of everything," I said.

Alex turned bright red. "I'm not like you, okay. I don't have the stomach for such things."

"Well I don't either, but I deal with it. At least you can eat the terrible meals they give us. At least you can stomach that." We sat for a while longer and I apologized for behaving so poorly. Then two frightening KGB officers asked us what we were doing. They did not smile. They were not friendly in the slightest. These were mean men, like the two drunks who assaulted my father. Or the drunk that turned me upside down. "We are playing," I told one of them. "You don't look like you are playing. Get out of here before we call your parents."

This was only the beginning of our encounters with the KGB. One night, the KGB banged on our door. My whole family awoke, trembling with fear. "What do they want now?" Mama said in a frightened voice. "What have we done?"

The banging became louder and louder with each knock. The sound of their fists on the metal door rocketed throughout the apartment walls, as Mama and Papa looked at each other in question.

Papa had no choice but to open the door. When he did, the KGB barged in screaming profanities at everyone they set their eyes upon. After a frightening inquisition, they realized that they were looking for another family and left us, angry that we'd taken up their time. Poor Misha cried and cried: "Papa! Why are those men so mean to us? Hold me please, I am so afraid."

After the KGB left, everyone was afraid to go back to bed, afraid that the KGB would return with more questions if they didn't find what they were looking for. This time, *we* could be the family they sought. No one could sleep that night. I heard my parents whispering in the other room. It sounded like something was definitely wrong. Shivering with fright, I spent the night hidden underneath my blanket and pillow.

Chapter Three

1974

December 31, 1974.

Glowing, with steam coming from it, the large copper teapot called *samovar* (which in Russian means "self-cooking") was receiving all the attention at our new kitchen table. Everyone around the table was waiting for a cup of tea. Everyone that is, except for my younger brother, Misha, and I. Comfy, snug and warm, this ten-year-old girl and her three-year old brother sat at the small window, hypnotized by the strange stillness outside. Other apartments were covered under the snow that looked like a huge, white blanket – what a sight! The only visible parts were the chimneys. Misha and I slid out of our beds, and went into the main room where family and guests had already gathered for a New Year's celebration.

The reason the samovar was so favoured was because of the cherished water boiling inside the container – water which takes about twenty to twenty-five minutes to boil. Mama was proficient in preparing samovar; Papa had no clue as to how to get it to work. The container must be filled with water. Then the metal tube in the middle of it was filled with crumpled newspaper and lit aflame. A dozen sticks of dry, thin wood were added to ignite the fire. Then charcoal was added. Mama would then puff and puff to keep it going.

Once the water reached the boiling point, the samovar was carried to the table and placed on a metal tray designed to protect the table from sparks and ashes of red-hot charcoal. With the samovar sitting proudly on the table steaming, puffing, singing to the surrounding company, and inviting all to partake of its generosity with prior troubles forgotten. The samovar still remains the darling of the traditional Russian table.

I recognized the faces gathered around the samovar, but not all of the names. Misha stood behind me and held on tightly to the bottom of my dress. He was not used to such a crowd. A guest of my father, with a salt and pepper beard, smiled warmly at me. His piercing blue eyes matched the collar of his shirt. He introduced himself as Alek, and he asked if my brother and I would like some sour cherries he brought from home. I smiled and nodded in delight. They were truly juicy and delicious. A real treat. Misha got cherry juice all over his face and hands.

As I washed Misha, Alek offered to help me. He rolled up his sleeves and I could see numbers tattooed on his forearm. Alek noticed me starting at his arm and then rolled his sleeve back down again. "Let's get this little gentleman clean," he told me in a low, raspy voice. I wanted to ask him about the tattoo, but even at the age of ten, I could sense Alek was uncomfortable about it.

I asked Papa about his friend Alek. I asked about his "numbers tattoo." Papa's face slowly turned into a pale white. I had never seen such an uncanny expression on Papa's face before. In fact, I do not think I had ever seen such an expression of terror on anyone's face before. "Do not ask about such things. I will tell you about that when you are a little older." This piqued my curiosity. Now I really wanted to know about the tattoo.

"Why? Is there something wrong with Alek? He is so nice, Papa. I'm old enough to know. Really, I am."

Papa was not one to lose his temper, but he raised his voice in a way I had never heard before. The whiteness of his face turned into a boiling red. "You are not old enough to know. Be a good girl and help your mother."

I helped Mama dutifully, and then later in the evening, my attention turned to Aunt Polina as she said something funny, raising her glass to a toast that someone had begun. I counted thirty-six people at the table – all adults. The children had to sit at a nearby table and could not speak to the adults unless spoken to first. I sat between my cousins Elaine and Marina, both two years older than me. Misha was unable to sit still for even a minute, constantly grabbing one thing or another from one of the two tables.

Even though Mama had put in eight hours of work, she was still busy in the kitchen finalizing dinner, but my grandmother was there to assist her. The two women were hastily making *borsht* and my maternal grandmother was making her famous *blintzes* and *vareniki* to impress family and guests.

After the toasts, some herring and vinaigrette (Russian salad) found its way to the table. Soon after, music began to fill the dining room, beginning with the traditional sounds of Red Army marches and Soviet hymns, and eventually switching to more enjoyable folk melodies.

As I sat quietly watching the samovar brewing, I overheard Mama's friends comment that I looked like a "mermaid" because of my head full of wavy, brown hair. Back then, my hair almost touched the floor when unbraided. It covered my whole body as if it were a long, silky gown. Mama's friends were forever suggesting that she cut off my wavy hair and sell it to them for wigs. I'm glad that my mother always refused… but I also knew that one day she would be forced to abide.

Papa put in more hours with Valarie, but the times were tough, and nobody had much money. We were hoping he could get a better drafting job or that my sister could get a job. Once we discussed this with Mama, and Lena offered to stop going to school for music, but Mama refused. "You are too gifted to stop schooling. You must continue."

Alla was no longer my friend, but she still lived next to me, and she was taking piano lessons from our neighbour down the street, Natalia Nicholaevna. She was a concert pianist, a strict teacher, though complimented by many families. One day, my mother and I went to her place to sign up for piano lessons.

I was ecstatic to finally be given a chance. For years I had dreamed of playing the piano like my sister Lena. Now we would finally have something to talk about. Lena would not talk about her secret books, so maybe I could bond with her over the piano.

We arrived at Natalia's house, and I made sure that my hair was brushed pristinely, and my face was washed well. After inspecting me from head to toe, the teacher told me to sit down at the piano. The shrill teacher played a short melody, then expected me to duplicate it right away. Not surprisingly, I was unsuccessful on both attempts I tried. She tolerated these attempts, and then announced to Mama that I not make a good student. She also said I would never make it into the conservatory no matter how hard I tried.

"But why?" Mama asked, devastated.

"Don't be too upset – not everyone is smart enough and good enough to be a pianist," Natalia replied, shaking her head. "Rebecca just wasn't born to be a musician. She can try and try, but she is simply not gifted like other girls. Please don't waste any more of my time and your time."

Then with a cold, artificial smile, she added, "besides – can't you tell your child is tone deaf!"

Mama noticed that the teacher was actually enjoying telling her this.

"She cannot be tone deaf," Mama insisted. "Rebecca knows all the notes, and even helps her friend Alla play scales."

I was very upset. *How dare she not even consider teaching me? After all, I can be as good as Alla, given a chance to prove.* But deep inside I knew the real reason why my friend was accepted, and I was not: Alla was not Jewish.

I acknowledged what the teacher said, that I was tone deaf and couldn't repeat the notes. But I desperately wanted to be a pianist like my older cousin, Lena.

Mama was still unconvinced and was shaking her head vigorously. "I simply don't believe it."

"Rebecca!" the teacher barked, "Play the C scale and I want you to sing each note for me."

Then the teacher looked at Mama. "Watch and hear for yourself! It's not enough to simply be able to hit the notes accurately, one must be able to recreate the sounds with one's voice and have good hearing."

I played and sang a note.

"Rebecca," the teacher barked again, "that is not a 'Mi' note. You sang a 'Fa' note – it is a false note. Repeat it at once again!" The teacher looked at Mama once again. "Now you hear why your daughter has no talent!"

I was now near tears, trying over and over to improvise as best I could. "Do – re – mi – fa – so – la – ti – do."

"Now, voice those notes backwards," the teacher, commanded.

"Do – ti – la – so – fa – mi – re – do." I sang and played.

"False notes!" she screamed. "I hear false notes! I do not want to hear 'FA' sharp in the C scale." By this time, even the teacher noticed I was crying. "Stop! No more. I heard enough!"

Turning to Mama she said, "as I was saying, a good musician must be able to reproduce the notes accurately, and Rebecca will always be lost during her exams at the conservatory. She is not able to improvise. So just forget the piano and conservatory. I don't see any talent in her." She closed the piano, and with a look of disdain said, "please go. I have another 'talented' pupil waiting for me."

Sadly, Mama and I got up and walked to the open doors. We knew that without a positive review from the respected teacher, I would never be given a chance to play in the Soviet Union.

It was at that point Mama made up her mind: we absolutely had to leave the country. Easier thought than done, since Soviet citizens needed special documents for all travel, even to visit their relatives in another city. A Soviet citizen had no right to change their place of residence without a special permit from the regional party office.

Mama, my sister and I sat down, and they tried to console me, but I cried and cried. It was not fair. The same story was playing out again and again. It was because we were Jewish that we had no opportunity.

As if the day was not bad enough, that same night, Papa came home and threw his apron on his chair resolutely. "Valarie told me there is no more work," he told us all. I did not even have ten minutes to feel bad about what happened with the piano. Now we all had to be sad for Papa.

Sometime later I ran into Alek at the market and he asked me how the family was. I could not get over how blue his eyes were. I told him that Papa lost his job, and that he needed something. Alek wrote something down on a piece of paper and told me to tell my Papa to meet him there at 7:30 pm. He said he was a member of a group that might be able to help.

I wanted to ask him about the tattoo on his arm again, but I decided not to. I thanked him and told Papa as soon as I arrived home. Mama, Lena, Misha, and I waited restlessly in the apartment for Papa to return home. Since losing his job at the market, and less and less work from his drafting job, Papa and Mama only had enough money to last us until the end of the month.

Mama mentioned that we could ask my father's grandfather for money, but Papa scoffed at the idea. "No matter what, I am going to take care of this family," he told us all in the living room.

Papa returned very late, perhaps around 11:00 pm and paced back and forth in our apartment. His footsteps were so heavy that the downstairs neighbour used a broom to hit the floor and tell us to be quiet. You could hear everything through the walls.

He sighed, sat in his chair, and nodded to himself. "Well?" said Mama. "What happened?" Papa rubbed his forehead, got up again, and turned on the radio so that the neighbours would not hear us. He blasted the state radio channel, and the broom again hit the floor, but we ignored his complaining.

"Alek is going to get me another job, this time at a meat packing facility, so I can bring home some good chicken for the family. But that's not the best news. The best news is that the group Alek is a prominent member of, is a dissident movement. He is organizing papers for his family to leave the country, and he says that we can leave too. It will just take some time, and of course more money."

I could not believe what I was hearing. I wondered if Alex was part of this same group. He had to be. The coincidence was too great. I asked him the very next day if his aunt Yana knew Alek. "Of course," said Alex. "Alek is important. Aunt Yana said Alek is one of the leaders of the group to get us out of here." It was astonishing to hear this.

I wanted to be part of the resistance, but I was only a little girl. Nobody took me seriously. I wanted to do something big, and I wanted to earn more money for the family so that we could leave Kiev sooner rather than later.

One day I heard Lena singing something quite strange outside our apartment building. She was singing something that was not quite classical. It was something I had never heard before. She was singing a wonderful folk song by Vladimir Semyonocivh Vysotsky. I was mesmerized by the sound. Lena sang louder, and I danced to the music. "See, I do have an ear for music," I told her. "I don't doubt it," said Lena. She was laughing, but not laughing at me. We were laughing together.

Lena stopped singing, and walked away, rather than to, our apartment. "Where are you going? It's almost time for dinner," I told her. "I'm going out," she said. Lena never went out, and I was not about to ask her where 'out' was. She would never take me. So, I followed her. I don't know what I was thinking, because Mama and Papa were expecting me. I also had responsibilities with Misha. But I felt it was unfair that Lena got to do whatever she wanted just because she was in music school, and nobody knew what was to become of me. I was tired of being good, and doing all my chores.

My sister walked a few blocks away, closer to the heart of the city. The Brezhnev Era became increasingly more modern and urban. Underground rock and folk concerts were beginning to pop up, and I was about to listen to my first one.

Lena lined up outside a bar, and I stood across the street watching her. There were people outside this bar selling blue jeans, just like the ones Yana wore. Bell bottoms, only they did not look as nice, as good, as the ones from the United States. I waited until my sister went inside, and then I stood outside this bar and asked one of the vendors how much he was selling the jeans for. "Its ten *kopeks* per pair," he told me. The boy must have been about fifteen years old.

"How much do you pay for them?" The boy scoffed at me. "If I told you that I wouldn't be a very good at business, now would I?" he said. I listened to the concert from outside, because I was too young to go to a bar. I also bought a pair of bell bottoms with what little money I had.

I went home before it was too late. I did not want to get in trouble. Before anybody could see me, I hid the bell bottoms under the mattress. My plan was to sell them for an even greater profit. I did sell them to a boy for fourteen *kopek*, and I stashed away my profit for later, to help Papa.

Papa was doing quite well in his new job. He brought home a full chicken now and then, a very nice thing to have for soup. Mama was so excited that she had the actual chicken breast, and not just the bones to make soup from. Naturally, I helped Mama, and fed the soup to Misha. I asked about Papa's friend Alek, but Papa said he could not speak of such things to me yet.

I would become frustrated when Papa spoke to me this way. I wanted to prove myself. When he sat in his chair, listening to the radio after dinner, I produced the fourteen *kopek* I had earned selling that pair of bell bottom jeans, and gave it to him. "This is so that we can go to Israel a little faster."

Papa laughed and kissed me on the forehead. "You are so lovely sometimes, my little Regoletta. Please keep that for yourself. I have a feeling we are going to run into good fortune soon." Papa's mood was unusually jovial, as it was towards the end of the week. Papa was usually quite tired from work. But, I was happy that Papa was happy.

Chapter Four

Country Life

My grandmother and grandfather received a piece of land, on the beautiful Dnieper River. It was upon this piece of land that Papa built a cottage (*dacha*) for us to live in during the summer. Around us were many other tiny cottages.

In the course of less than a year, we had gone from worrying about how to pay the bills, to the luxury of escaping city life. The apartment had become suffocating, and I was so excited to travel, quite rare in Ukraine during this time. Travelling required the proper paperwork. Luckily my father's friend Alek was able to provide us with what we needed.

I was still so curious about Alek, and wanted to know more about how they met. My father never wanted to talk about it, and I would soon find out why.

The acreage greeted us with bare land, with the potential of bearing apple trees and pear trees. An extraordinary benefit to us; the fertile land greatly impressed my grandmother.

With a lot of help from my uncles and cousins, our family soon had a new dacha. Even though it was rather small, one big room and a small kitchen, our dacha had a large veranda. I would enjoy sitting on this veranda and singing with my sister Lena. We sang some of the new folk songs, and I promised not to tell Mama and Papa that she snuck out to these places to listen to music.

Our kitchen had nothing more than a Primus stove, a few shelves for pots and pans, a lot of boxes on the floor, and a cold cellar. Papa painted the dacha green and installed big square windows. The stove-hearth, called *pechka,* was installed to keep the warmth in our dacha.

Unfortunately, the washroom was an outhouse. Inside was an oval hole carved out of a wooden plank. On the wall of the cubicle was a long, thick nail, with dozens of newspaper pieces serving as toilet paper. There was no running water. My job was to fetch pails of water from the nearby communal well, and dump it into the self-made water container.

We brought in wooden beds from a neighbouring town just a few miles away. This was followed by the arrival of mattresses and pillows for the beds.

My grandparents had specific plans for the dacha; my grandfather set up a hammock to sleep under the apple tree, while my grandmother planted a variety of fruit and vegetables in the garden. A garden they could finally call their own.

My family walked to the nearby town of Arsenal, which was located in the woods, to buy something to eat. Upon reaching Arsenal's bazaar, we saw an abundance of vegetables and fruit. The bazaars were filled with hefty mounds of juicy, round melons, and golden honeydews. Peppers, eggplant, tomatoes, and cucumbers were available and offered by the surrounding *sovkhozes.* As plentiful as the fruit and vegetables were, they were very expensive. Only watermelons, through the whole season, were inexpensive enough for us to enjoy on a regular basis. Dnieper apples, pears, and cherries were easily obtainable. But things such as grapes, although grown in profusion, were extremely expensive, and considered to be truly a treat. Dairy products such as cheeses, particularly *brynza* or feta, were difficult to find. But Russians savoured fish, especially dry, salty fish called (*taranka*) and caviar, considered a delicacy.

When everything was prepared, the Russian tradition was to sit and celebrate with food and alcohol. The new neighbours were invited, and everyone gathered around the big table for a feast. There were bottles of sweet liqueurs, heavy liqueur and *Kvas* (traditional Russian drink) for non-drinkers. Most Russian men generally favoured vodka, while some women liked drinking to keep their men company. Women generally preferred sherry or red wine.

There were also diverse dishes with food and meat pies, *cholodetz*, herring, vinaigrette salad (Russian potato salad), beet salad with thickly sliced rye bread and caviar, and bowls of marinated mushrooms (another Russian treat). As for the sweets – there were tarts and a variety of cookies, candies and ice cream.

When my family received letters from relatives or friends, all the letters were intercepted, opened, and the contents were censored. If approved, they were glued back together and sent on their way to the receiver. If the government did not approve of the contents, then the letters were destroyed.

It was the same thing with the phone calls – they were all monitored. And not everyone had a phone. For each person who had and used one, the government had officials listening to every word on the other side. If something anti-Russian was stated, the phone connection was lost and the people would not be able to reconnect for some time.

This is why it astounded me that Papa was willing and able to listen to his secretive radio back home. To be honest, it worried Mama that we had just left it in the apartment. If the KGB would have walked in, it could have been discovered. Luckily, it was not. We were able to enjoy our wonderful dacha in peace.

As I fetched the water. I took in the country life. I wished I could just stay in this blissful existence until we moved to Israel. How I longed for that day of freedom.

When I returned to our dacha, I saw Alek sitting with my father again. I thought this was finally my chance to know more about him. They were chatting, and Alek greeted me warmly like he always had. He invited me to sit with them as they conversed on the veranda, and took in the beautiful country landscape. I could tell my father was uncomfortable, but Alek reassured him. "Let her sit with us," he told my father.

Mama was busy cleaning, and Lena was helping with Misha, so I was wonderfully free to sit with Papa and Alek. "How did you become friends?" I asked Alek. My father snapped. "Rebecca. What did I tell you about asking Alek such questions?" Alek frowned. He looked at me carefully then turned his attention to Papa. "I think we should tell her. I think she should know."

My father cleared his throat, which was very unlike him. He began developing unusual nervous habits, because of the enormous pressure he was under. He was constantly worried about work, money, feeding the family, and most importantly of all, our safety. Our safety was not guaranteed during this time, which many North American Jews of today find it difficult to comprehend. "Fine, Alek. Tell her. I can't."

Alek rolled up his sleeve and showed me the tattoo I had seen before. The one I was so curious about. "These are the numbers the Nazis tattooed on me when I was in the concentration camp. You see, Rebecca in Kiev, there is great hatred towards the Jewish people. Your people. It's plain as day, and right now it looks as though this hatred is getting worse. I know what it's like when people do terrible things to each other out of hate." Alek's blue eyes were squinting now. He was remembering something that appeared to be quite painful.

"When I was a little boy in the camp, I thought that I would die. Indeed, I could see my own ribcage, and I was close to starving to death. I had accepted death, but then, as I lay in my bunk about to leave this earth, I thought I should see the stars for the last time. I mustered all my strength and snuck outside the bunk."

"I knew I could have been shot by the Nazi guards, but I did not care. I just leaned up against the outside wooden wall of the bunker, and looked at the brilliantly white stars in the night sky. Suddenly, I heard footsteps, and I closed my eyes. I was ready to be shot by a Nazi. I thought for sure, these footsteps must be that of a Nazi guard. I sat and sat, in terrifying anticipation, and then I felt something drop into my lap. It was a potato, and that potato was given to me by your father. I saw him standing above me, wearing tattered stripes, just like the ones I was wearing. The stripes of a Jewish prisoner."

I could not believe the story. I was wondering if Alek was serious. I also knew that Papa did not have a tattoo. He had a large scar on his arm, but no tattoo. "If you were in the camp, then why don't you have a tattoo like Alek, Papa?" This was a harsh thing to say in hindsight, but I was direct. I was deeply curious.

Papa cleared his throat again in the same nervous way as before. He rolled down his sleeve and showed me the scar that

I was familiar with. "I burned it off, with an iron," he told me. "I could not stand to look at it."

We sat on the veranda in silence. I was in shock. Alek looked so calm compared to Papa. He seemed to be impervious to all the suffering this country inflicted on the Jewish people. I also wondered why Papa had to burn the tattoo off, but Alek did not. I wondered about this for years afterwards. Perhaps an explanation was that Papa could not stand to be reminded by the tattoo, while Alek did not mind, because the tattoo served as a reminder of his perseverance over such an evil force. It reminded him of how he survived, like a scar would remind one of a cut that healed.

"I know how bad it can get for us. Your father also knows this. I'm surprised you never told her Vladimir," Alek remarked to my father.

My father got up and started pacing again. He could not sit still. "I don't want to remember those days, Alek. I just, can't." Alek nodded his head. "Yes, I understand."

"You are the only one who can understand," said Papa. Alek shifted in his chair and he changed the subject.

"Zev in New York is still working out big picture solutions with the embassy. We want all Soviet Jews who want to make Aliyah to be able to do so. The political situation seems like it is changing. There seems to be an impending motivation to increase diplomatic ties with the United States, by allowing Jews to emigrate. We have to act now, and we have quite a lot of work to do."

Alek was a highly intelligent man. I could tell by the way he spoke not only to Papa, but to me as well. He was one of the few adults who I felt was truly listening to me. I was fascinated by this man.

The next day, Alek left and told Papa that they would be in touch soon. Our family stayed for a while longer, enjoying the beautiful weather. All of the jobs being created in the city led to mass unemployment in the agricultural sector. Most villages were very poor, and I saw this poverty firsthand as I went to fetch water.

A boy about my age came up to me without shoes on. He wanted to know if I could give him a blanket for warmth. I did not want to lead him back to my family, so I told him that we had no blankets for him, and that my father was KGB. He left me in peace after I told him this.

Alas, we eventually had to leave country life, and my grandparents were particularly sad when they heard this news. "The city is such a cruel place," remarked my grandfather. "It is full of hatred towards Jews."

Chapter Five

Occupations

Brezhnev's time (1964-1982) was different than the Stalin era (1922-1953) in many ways. One way it was different was that during Stalin's time, a common worker could expect a promotion if they studied hard and obeyed authority. In the time I lived, this was not the case. Professionals like my father held onto their positions for dear life and never wanted to leave.

The political system made it so that people couldn't be fired for incompetence. It's something that didn't bother Papa too much, but it bothered Mama.

She complained often about her coworkers. To make matters worse, she was also tired having to do the majority of the housework, and take care of three children. Lena did not clean the house as much as she should have. I was only ten years old and did more work than Lena.

My father began mentioning the names of some Soviet Jewish intellectual leaders, like Anatoly Sharanksy, Larisa Bogaraz, and others. They spoke openly about their desire to leave the Soviet Union for Israel.

I asked Alex if he wondered what Israel would be like. "I just hope it is better than here," he told me. "I just don't want to be bullied for being Jewish anymore." I felt the same way. We knew very little about Israel at the time, but for some reason we felt as though it were home. It was a place where we could be safe from persecution and discrimination. An oasis, waiting for us.

When I arrived home, I found that my beloved sister Lena was in tears. I was surprised to see her this way. I could not remember the last time I saw her cry. There was a letter on the kitchen table. I read the letter as Mama consoled her.

After a child completes grade 10, the KGB instructs them on what kind of occupation they are going to have. Lena completed ten grades of the Royal Conservatory of Music. She wanted to go to university and continue her studies in piano. The KGB's letter said her application had been denied. The reason was simple: she was Jewish.

I tried to make Lena feel better, but at this time we did not have the relationship we have today. She told me all she wanted to do was cry, and to leave her alone. For two weeks, she did not leave the apartment. She cried and cried, and did not even have the strength to play the piano. In fact, she never played the piano again. She began drinking, and this bothered my parents greatly.

There were many times over the next few months I tried to make Lena feel better, but she became mean towards me. She called me names, and I did not like that at all. Mama said not to take it personally, and that Lena was just going through a phase. Eventually she had to get over her sorrow, and she took a work placement in an office as a secretary. Such a waste of talent.

I wondered what my occupation would be. I was still so young, and that decision was far away. Little did I know that by the time I would finish grade ten, I would already be gone from Kiev. Gone from the USSR. I was quite fortunate in this way.

It was also getting crowded in our little apartment. My sister needed her own space, and during the same time she began work as a secretary, Mama began looking for a husband for my sister.

Lena did not like most of the men Mama suggested. We sat over the kitchen table, looking at their photographs. It was so exciting. I told them who I thought was cute and who I thought was not very cute. They hushed me, but I gave my opinion anyway.

Lena was so picky. The man who showed up at our apartment truly stunned me. He was not very good looking at all. He was quite rude. And he certainly did not look Jewish at all. The reason he did not look Jewish was because he wasn't. His name was Igor. He was a construction worker, and I did not think he had anything in common with Lena.

They dated for quite some time. Igor picked up Lena on his motorcycle, which was obnoxiously loud, and was quite rude to Papa and Mama. One day they left on a date and Mama began to cry. "I don't know why she did this to us. She used to be such a nice girl. Now she is with this guy, and it's as though she's a different person. I don't like it. I don't like this at all."

It all happened so fast. Within the span of weeks my sister dated, and then married this man, and we knew nothing about him. There was no Jewish wedding. No Jewish rituals. It was as though we had lost a family member.

At the time, I was quite angry with her. The entire family was angry with Lena. Now I feel sad that it happened the way it did. We did not understand how truly crushing it was to not be able to play the piano. Lena once said to me, "I don't like most of what he is, but we can sing together sometimes. For me, that's enough. I need to feel like I can share my love for music with someone, otherwise life is not worth living."

Some Jewish people married non-Jews to hide their true identity. Some of them were embarrassed to be Jewish, and actually renounced their faith. Lena took Igor's last name, so that her name did not sound Jewish. I do not think Lena was embarrassed to be Jewish. I think she was tired of carrying the burden.

Papa did not say much about what happened. He kept things bottled inside. Mama was more vocal. She became depressed at this situation. It was hard for her to accept. I vowed to myself that I would never give up who I was. I would never give up my identity no matter what. I had suffered too much in my ten short years to allow that to happen.

Shortly after this event, the promise I had made to myself would be tested. I arrived one day at school to find that Alex was absent. I asked Mrs. Berdichevsky where Alex was, and she snickered at me. "How should I know?" She scoffed. I asked some of the other children if they saw him and nobody would say. I had no friends in this school. My only friend was Alex. I had not spoken to Alla since we fought, and I was not about to start.

To my surprise, she came to me in the cafeteria. She sat next to me which was a big no- no. But she sat next to me with her new friend, Nina. "Alex is in Siberia now," she told me. "He's swimming with the polar bears."

"No, he's not," I shouted at Alla. Alla smiled in a way that terrified me. I recognized that evil smile on Mrs. Berdichevsky, our principal, and the thugs on the street. It was the same seething hatred that I was so familiar with. "Yes, he is. His father was caught with an American. They called him a Zionist scum, and they sent the whole family to Siberia. Nina can tell you that, because Nina's dad is KGB. Nina told me, and now I'm telling you," said Alla.

I was physically sick. I ran to the bathroom to throw up, but I had no food in my mouth. I did not eat the cafeteria food, so the acid burned my throat. I cried and cried in the bathroom, and I heard Alla and Nina laughing at me.

To think that this was true was terrifying. I had to believe that they were just making up a story, and I wondered if my father would know anything about Alex and his family. I asked my father as soon as he came home from work. "I don't know. There is no way for me to find out. You need to leave this alone, Rebecca. Don't say anything to that Nina girl or to Alla. Just ignore them."

I had to visit Alex at his house and see for myself. As I approached his family's house, I saw that it was empty. The door was kicked in, and the meagre belongs they had, had been taken or looted. My best friend was gone, and I could not say anything. I could not go back home to Mama or Papa.

Instead I went to my grandparents, Papa's parents, who were very religious. I burst into their home and I cried and cried. "I just don't understand why it has to be this way. Why is it so hard to be who we are? Why does everyone hate us so much?" My grandfather hugged me. He held me on his lap, and he kissed me on the forehead the way Papa did to make me feel better.

"Rebecca, we cannot know the will of G-d. All I can say, is that he has a plan for us. We must not lose sight of the light in this dark time. G-d will provide a way. He always has. As for your friend, we simply do not know. If it is G-d's will that they find their way to Siberia, then there is nothing we can do. We must accept this. We must pray for their safety and for their health."

I prayed with my grandfather for Alex and his family. Somehow it did not make me feel better. I felt worse, perhaps even more helpless than before. My grandmother and grandfather gave me some soup. That made me feel better. I was hungry and dehydrated. But now, I was also terribly sad and I would be sad about Alex for some time.

The next day I was waiting in a queue for bread, and I overheard a conversation. I was looking down.

I was depressed about Alex, and the men in front of me were talking about politics. "To be honest, I don't care who wins and who loses. Khrushchev was bad, and Brezhnev is just as bad. I just want to have my day off and I want to drink."

The second man turned to the first man. "I couldn't agree more. Cheers to Brezhnev, or whoever it is."

There was no such thing as patriotism. People did not care. The atmosphere was that of helplessness and defeat. Perhaps this was one of the reasons the Jewish people did not succumb to alcoholism like most Ukrainians. We always tried. We always thought of ways to make things better for ourselves and for our people. Alek was working to bring the Jewish people to Israel. My father was also working to this end.

We had some semblance of hope, which was more than most people. We also cared about the politics. We were aware of the politics, which made us even more aware of our goal: to get out of this place, before they began to kill us.

The line up to get bread was over two hours long. Then I was turned away, so I had to leave and get into another line that was two hours. This was all after school, and so by the time I got home, it was well past dinner. I tore off a piece of bread and cut the bread into little cubes for Misha to eat. He had an enormous smile on his face. And he kissed me when I fed him more. His smile gave me so much strength, that I ended up feeding him my share.

During the time I lived with my parents, which is to say the Brezhnev Era, the average income per head increased. This did not mean we were better off during Brezhnev than we were during Khruschev's time (1953-1964). In fact, we were perhaps worse off. The 1965 Soviet economic reform, sometimes called the Kosygin reform and the push for decentralization, had effects that did not necessarily benefit all workers equally.

As I mentioned before, there was incompetence in professional jobs such as my father's, and blue-collar workers like bus drivers were sometimes paid even more than professionals. My father actually made the same salary at the meat packing plant as he did as a draftsman.

I watched my little brother fall asleep, and I thought about my sister Lena. Then I thought about what kind of occupation I would go into when I became of age. I thought the only one I was interested in was taking care of children. I really wanted my own family, and a wonderful husband to take care of me. It was all so clear to me then. I fell asleep with my little brother Misha in my arms. When I thought about taking care of children, suddenly I felt as though I would not care about the pay.

There were more meetings between Papa and his friend Alek. Alek spoke about Natan Sharanksy, who was the leader of the Zionist movement inside the Soviet Union, who demanded full religious and cultural rights for Jews. He also spoke about Andrei Sakharov and other human rights activists.

I loved listening to their conversations, late into the night while the radio played. With my sister now gone, and my mother always tired, I took on responsibility for more housework. My job was to take care of the home and to take care of Misha and my Papa. I loved to do this work. But I also needed a creative outlet. It still stung me that the teachers said I did not have an ear for music. It caused me to remember another discouraging comment made, that my hearing was like "an elephant stepped on my ear."

Despite these terribly demeaning remarks, I decided that I would teach myself music. Lena left all her notes from school in our apartment, and I collected them and read them whenever I had time.

Then I drew a keyboard on a couple sheets of paper lined up in a row, and practiced by pressing on the drawn-on keys. Mama walked in on me one day and watched me practice. "What are you doing?" she asked me. "I'm practicing piano," I said. Mama gave me a big hug. "You can do anything you set your mind to. Don't listen to that silly music teacher. Don't listen to Alla. Don't listen to anyone who will discourage you from your dream. You are so strong, Rebecca. I am very proud of you."

I did feel very good about playing my imaginary piano; however, I do not believe I actually improved, as there was no way to tell. Instead, I only dreamed about a time when I could play a real piano.

One day I became quite ill. Due to my erratic eating schedule, my stomach eventually gave up, and I could not keep any food down. I lost even more weight. My skin turned yellow, and Mama had to take me to the hospital.

I could no longer perform my daily chores, or wait in long line ups for bread. Astonishingly, the USSR had the highest physician to patient ratio in the world, but many doctors could not perform basic tasks, like reading an electrocardiogram.

As we waited in the waiting room, a doctor arrived by bicycle. Something was wrong with his bicycle, and he attempted to fix the chain in front of us. He tried turning one screw and then another, and a component of the bike ended up becoming wedged in the wheel. He actually made the problem worse. I hoped that this man was not my doctor. That was my hope.

Dr. Kostenko was indeed the doctor who could not fix his own bicycle. He told Mama that I was malnourished and needed to take vitamins, and consume a liquid diet for a week. I was relieved nothing was seriously wrong with me, but I was unsure as to whether this doctor knew what he was talking about.

Luckily Dr. Kostenko was correct, but then our refrigerator broke, and this was a terrible thing to have happened. We were fortunate enough to own a refrigerator, but most of the country did not. In the early mid to late 1970s, only two thirds of Soviet families had a refrigerator. The US hit two thirds in the early 1930s. Soviet families had to wait years to get one, and they had a one hour window to pick it up. They lost their chance if they did not arrive on time.

We could not afford to wait that long for a new refrigerator, so we filled the fridge with ice while Papa searched for someone who was skilled enough to repair the fridge.

Shortly after our refrigerator broke, a pianist came to my school. She was Jewish, and one year older than I was, which made me feel over the moon with joy. I had missed my dear friend Alex for quite some time, and I was relieved to have some social interaction with another Jewish student. Her name was Sofa.

Sofa's father was a mechanic, and since we became friends, he offered to fix our refrigerator for free, in exchange for some of my mother's wonderful cooking. "My wife can't cook at all," said Mr. Vovk, jokingly.

Sofa was fun to hang out with, but she was not as talented as my sister was at playing the piano. She also did not have the ability to teach me. Instead she wanted to go out, and she introduced me to her friends who went to different schools.

Finally, I was going to have a social life. I was suffocated before, but just thinking that made me feel guilty about Alex. I was still sick with worry about what happened to him, and worried whether the KGB could come for us too. The thought even crossed my mind that I should destroy my father's radio, so that the KGB would not be able to find it. I dismissed this thought. It was more important to be privy to any important information.

Sofa was only a year older than me, but all of her friends were older than her by a couple years. As a result, I was the youngest in my new group of Jewish friends. Between school, our training and taking care of the groceries for Mama, I did not have much free time for socialization. I stayed up very late, however, because I longed to be with girls and boys my own age. My nature was to be extroverted, and I was starved for this interaction without my only friend Alex.

Sofa introduced me to two other girls, Marta and Maria. Marta was thirteen and she lived close to me. Maria was twelve and she lived closer to Sofa. We all met at the bazaar that served as a halfway point.

We were only children, but we repeated the politics that our parents spoke about. Jewish people, and even children, were far more interested in politics. We had an interest in what went on, because there were serious consequences for us.

Brezhnev introduced the policy of *rastsvet*, *sblizhenie*, and *sliiani*. These terms meant flowering, drawing together, and merging together. The idea was to unite all Soviet nationalities into one. This was perhaps nice in theory, but never worked in practice.

"My father said that *sliiani* is nothing but the Russification policy that Khrushchev came up with," said Marta. Marta had unusual red hair and freckles. In a way, this was bad, because she was heavily bullied. But in another was this was also good, because nobody suspected that she was Jewish.

I was still getting to know her. She was the best speaker of the group. Her father was a doctor. I did not understand what she was saying at the time about Khrushchev. I would later learn that he was one of the leaders before Brezhnev.

I would also learn that the Russification policy was the promise of communism in 20 years. This was a slogan that was said by Nikita Khrushchev at the end of the twenty second Congress of the Communist Party of the Soviet Union in 1961. He believed that twenty years was the time it took to build a truly communist society. This was of course not true, and could be traced all the way back to Vladimir Lenin.

Vladimir Lenin had a vision that when the Soviet Union would reach the final stage of communism, we would also reach the final stage of human development. Brezhnev now spoke frequently on the radio about what was called "developed socialism," and I asked Marta what she thought this term meant. She did not know, and promised to ask her father.

Maria's father had a job very similar to my father's. He was a draftsman, and I asked her if she also had a table in her living room? "Yes," she told me. "How did you know?" "Because my father has the same profession," I told her. The Jewish people always tried to educate themselves as much as possible. This is one reason why a lot of Soviets hated us, but also the reason we were able to later escape.

We would joke with one another at the bazaar, and Maria and Marta liked to talk about boys. I kept silent, but they asked me if there was anybody as school who I liked. "I liked this boy named Alex, but he was taken away from the KGB."

Marta raised her red-haired eyebrow at me. "I don't know if you are kidding or not," she told me. "I'm not kidding," I said. Sofa gave me a hug. "It will be okay, Rebecca. We don't know if he was taken away. It's just a suspicion." I did not say anything. I was still very upset about Alex.

Marta told us she asked her dad what real socialism was, and he laughed out loud. "What is real socialism? You want to know what that is, Marta? It's when you cannot buy what you need without money. Then if you get money, it's when you still cannot buy what you need."

In reality, this "real socialism" Brezhnev was speaking about on the radio was nothing more than an ideological catchphrase. It was a kind of economic planning that argued that this kind of "real" economic planning was needed for the country to succeed in the world. The reality was quite the opposite, as Marta's father pointed out in his terrible joke. It did not conform to the Marxist concept of socialism, and people mocked Brezhnev in private. At least those who knew what was going on did so, in secret, of course.

Nobody paid attention to the voices of little girls, no less the voices of little *Jewish* girls, so were safe to speak as we pleased, although quietly and beneath the din of the bustling bazaar.

We were living in the "Era of Stagnation" a term was coined by Gorbachev after Brezhnev had died in 1982. After Brezhnev, there was Yuri Andropov. After him was Konstantin Chernenko. After him was Mikhail Gorbachev. All these names in history mean very little unless you've lived through it. What I lived through was a time of great suffering. The Soviets hated the Jewish people, and a lot of it had to do with economics as well. The worse the economy did, the worse our people were treated. Gorbachev, of course, blamed Brezhnev for everything in later years, but this was politics. The reason Brezhnev came to power was because the perception was that the man before him was not good for the economy. And so, it goes.

Maria, Marta, Sofa, and I became close friends because we had to. We needed each other to survive such a hateful environment, both socially and politically, not to mention financially. Our parents began to become friends. It started when Sofa's father fixed our refrigerator. Then Maria's father and my father began speaking, because they were both draftsmen.

Some time later, Papa broke a piece of his drafting table, and swore. There was nowhere to go to fix such a specialized piece of equipment. Fortunately, I knew Maria, and I told him that Maria's father was also a draftsman. Mark was Maria's father, and the two of them sat and spoke for a while. Mama gave them a plate of herring to munch on.

"You have such a smart daughter," Mark told Papa. "Thank you," I said. Papa also thanked Mark for the lovely compliment. "I can't thank you enough for helping me with this. I don't know how I would have done it without you," Papa told Mark. "Well, perhaps you can thank me with some herring, if you have," said Mark.

Mama loved herring It was a wonderful and salty fish to eat, but it was very hard to get at the market, and it was expensive as well. A real treat. Non-Jews would prefer something like vodka. Drinking was a cultural activity for non-Jewish people in the country at the time.

Papa and Mark talked about their work, and they did complain about the incompetent co-workers they were stuck with. "My apprentice is being paid more than I am," Mark complained to Papa. "An apprentice! I have worked at my firm for over eight years, and this is the thanks I get. Why? Because I am Jewish, that's why."

Papa asked me to leave, and I thought I knew the reason why, but I could not be sure. I imagined Papa was talking to him about the impending plan to move a large number of Jews to out of the country. I was told to go out and play, and although Maria or Marta were not available, I did find Sofa.

"What do you hope to be when you reach grade ten?" I asked my friend. Sofa was very pretty. She had long, straight black hair and delicate features with a perfectly straight nose. She did not look stereotypically Jewish. Sofa thought about it, and told me she was thinking about studying piano.

I told her about what happened to Lena. I told her the tragic tale and this seemed to discourage her, which was the opposite of what I intended. "Please don't let me discourage you from trying," I said. "I just want to let you know what happened to my sister. Because she was Jewish, they did not let her play. But if you want to do it, you should try. Nobody believed in me, and I still try."

Sofa hugged me. She was a very affectionate friend. She had a good heart. I worried again that I had discouraged her. Then she asked me what I wished my occupation could be. "To be honest, I want to raise a family. I don't want to be a secretary. I don't want to work for the party. My love is for children."

I became closer with Sofa, because we went to the same school. We were still bullied because of being Jewish, but because we stuck together the taunting happened less.

It wasn't just bullying either. Mr. Kulic began to touch Sofa's hair quite inappropriately. He got too close to her, and we both worried that he was going to assault her. I told Sofa to always stick by me, and she agreed. This frustrated Mr. Kulic, and he yelled at me often, for no particular reason. I was of course I was used to this. I did not let his rude remarks dissuade me from sticking by my friend.

But I could not stop it from happening, no matter how hard I tried. Sofa began crying next to me in the cafeteria one day. I asked her to tell me what was wrong, but she wouldn't say. She told me she would tell me after school.

On our walk home, she told me that Mr. Kulic had violated her in the small room where he had beaten me. I asked her for details, but she would not give them to me. All she said was that "he kept touching me." Then she began to cry again.

I was so angry that this happened to my dear friend. How could such an animal exist? I had to do something. I had to tell someone, but Sofa insisted that I kept quiet.

"How! How can you keep quiet when he behaved like that towards you?" I was furious, and Sofa begged me to keep my voice down. "I need to tell someone. He needs to be held accountable." Sofa clawed at my arm. She drew blood from my skin with her fingernails. I could not believe it this was happening.

"Nobody will believe me. Nobody will take the word of a Jewish girl over that of Mr. Kulic. Please, just don't say anything to anyone."

That evening I was not myself. Mama and Papa noticed. Even little Misha noticed and began to cry. I told them that I had forgotten to buy bread for supper. "Forgotten? How could you have forgotten? You buy bread every week at the same time," Mama told me. It was true, it was a terrible excuse. Still, I was so upset that I could not respond. "I will go out now to buy bread," I told Mama.

As I waited in line, another bum asked me for *kopeks* to buy alcohol. I spat in his face, and he violently turned me upside down, shook all the money out of my pockets and stole my money. I cried in line, but someone took pity on me. It was Valarie, the grocer who fired my father.

"I'm sorry, little girl. Take some bread free of charge. I am sorry that happened to you." I knew that Valarie was a good man. I wanted to know the reason why he fired my father, but I thought this might be pushing my luck. Everything was a struggle. Nothing in this life was easy. I learned this lesson at such a young age. One must fight for everything in this life.

The worst part about what happened to my friend Sofa was that the ordeal was only beginning. Mr. Kulic would assault her regularly, and she was not herself after the incident. She became withdrawn and cold. This only became worse with the incidents that followed.

One day her father came to our apartment to speak to Papa. I arrived home to find Mark visibly upset. Papa was tired from work and did not want to be bothered, but his disposition changed when he realized how upset Mark was. My mother offered Mark some food, but he declined.

"Ah, little Rebecca, it is so nice to see you," said Mark. He was not sitting still. He was fidgeting with his hands and tapping on the floor with his boot. Mark looked very nervous. "I was wondering if you can tell me something about Sofa. She hasn't been herself and you are her best friend. Just a week ago she was such a happy child, but now all she does is stay in her room. She will not even tend to the chores. We haven't the slightest idea what's wrong. She won't talk to us."

I became very uncomfortable. I could not speak directly to Mark, so I turned to Papa and asked him as tentatively as I could. "Papa, Sofa told me not to say why she feels sad," I said. Papa nearly exploded with rage. Again, this was not like Papa. Only recently had he begun to behave this way. The stress of our situation was beginning to take its toll on Papa. "Rebecca, you must tell Mark what you know. It's not proper for you to keep secrets. Sofa is unwell."

I tried to explain that it was a secret again, but I did not have the words. I was just too frightened, but I also wanted Sofa to be helped, so I told Mark what I knew. As soon as Mark heard this, the blood rushed from his face. He demanded to know the name of the teacher. I told him with my head bowed low.

"Go away now," Mark told me, quite rudely. Papa looked at me and nodded. This was the worst news a father could possibly hear.

I could not imagine the thoughts running through Mark's mind at that moment. It would not take very long before I found out.

Sofa and I were seated in Mr. Kulic's class in the front row when it happened. Mr. Kulic was writing something on the chalkboard when Mark burst through the door in a rage.

We were all shocked to see him barge into the classroom in the way that he did. Mark was in a rage unlike I anything I had ever seen. His face was red, his fists were clenched. He looked at Mr. Kulic and asked him if he was the scum that touched his daughter. Mr. Kulic's hands were by his side. He slowly backed himself into the chalkboard. There was nowhere to hide. "I…I…I don't know what you are talking about," said Mr. Kulic. Mark slowly walked toward Mr. Kulic and asked him again, in a lower voice.

"Are you, or are you not Mr. Kulic? Are you Sofa's math teacher?" Mr. Kulic's eyes were wide with terror. He was thinking about what to say, but he could not say no. He had to admit it. "Yes. Now what is the meaning of this disruption?"

Mark did not respond. He wound up and punched Mr. Kulic as hard as he could in the face. Mr. Kulic fell to the ground and the whole class erupted in cheers and screams. Principal Boyko ran from his office to Mr. Kulic's classroom.

"What is the meaning of this? Who is this man?" Sofa was beside me the entire time, she was crying. We were both terrified about what was going to happen next. When members of the militia came to investigate the matter, they immediately knew who was in the right and who was in the wrong. There was no question. Sofa's parents were to be exiled to Siberia. This time there was no doubt in my mind.

This happened with lightning speed. We were not living in a democracy. There were no "fair rules." Mark was a Jew who assaulted a gentile teacher with ties to the KGB. It did not matter what the reason was. Within a couple days, Sofa no longer had any parents. She was an orphan child.

I begged Mama and Papa to take her in. "We don't have the money to support another child," said Mama. "We barely have enough to support ourselves." This news made me feel quite ill. "Well, what is to happen to Sofa? What will become of her?"

I would learn through the mail what happened to Sofa. She sent me a letter from a home for orphaned children, where she now lived. All letters were read by the KGB, so she could not say how terrible it was, but I could see the tear stains on the stationary she used. I could read in between the lines. Her life was over, and I felt terrible. I felt a tremendous amount of guilt for what happened to Sofa. I spoke with Papa about it, and he told me that there was nothing I could do. "As long as we are discriminated against, we have to know we are in a disadvantaged position. Accordingly, we must not let emotions get the better of us. What happened to her is terrible, but we cannot do anything about it. We must move on," he said, almost in tears.

"What does that mean, Papa? I can't just move on." I said. "We have no choice," Papa lamented.

My father now hid the radio under the mattress because there were spies everywhere. The events of recent weeks had made my parents nervous. More Jews were being exiled, and there were more violent attacks on us in the street. The economic situation was worsening by the day. These attacks were completely unprovoked, and they were horrific.

Papa sat in his chair. He cleared his throat and he concentrated on his drawings to ease his mind. I watched his hand made clean, unwavering lines on the paper. Without lifting his gaze, he addressed me.

"Rebecca, you may feel this rage, like the rage Mark felt when he learned what happened to Sofa. You may feel it, and you may think about it. But you must never act so cavalierly. It does not matter that you are in the right. In the end, the Soviets will hurt you far worse than you can ever hurt them. If we want to fight back, we must do it smartly."

Chapter Six

A Bag Full of Apples

I WANTED TO LEARN MORE about Papa's time in the concentration camp. I was very curious, because the only story I ever heard from that time was from Alek. My father insisted that he did not want to talk about it, and I did not bring it up again.

I was, however, looking forward to the next time I would see Alek, because then I would just ask him instead. Sometimes I was a mischievous child, but this came from a strong instinct to rebel and survive. The last time I saw Alek was when we traveled to the country, but that seemed so long ago now. I pined to go back to those days.

Every day the economic situation got worse, and now, despite the fact that my father had two jobs, and my mother worked, the money was not enough. I thought that if I could not get a job, then I would learn as much as I possibly could about the communist party. My friends Maria and Marta were highly intelligent, and I wanted to learn from them. I learned from my father from a young age that it is important to surround yourself with people who are smarter than you. This advice was so true and important.

I sat in Maria's kitchen one day, and her mother made us tea. Marta was also there, but we were all still upset about Sofa. I was thankful that they did not blame me for what happened. For a while, I was nervous that they would.

"I can't believe that Sofa is no longer with us," said Maria's mother. "Does anyone know where her parents went?" Maria's mother asked this to all of us. I told her that I knew they had been exiled to Siberia. Maria's mother nearly dropped the tray of tea she brought for us.

Marta asked Maria's mother, Yulana, about Siberia. Yulana sat down with us, and told us to "please put a lump or two of sugar in our tea and enjoy that first," before she spoke. She cleared her throat, and then did not say anything. "I wonder if I should even tell you," she said to us all. "Please tell us," I said to Yulana.

"Very well," said Yulana. "The camps in Siberia are not much better than the concentration camps under the Nazis. Many people die there. They die from the cold and they die from being overworked and underfed. If you think we do not have enough to eat here, try making it in a Siberian work camp."

Maria asked her mother how she knew this. "My sister, your aunt Dina was sent there. That's how I know. I have never told you how Dina died, but she died in Siberia." Maria's mother began to cry. Maria consoled her mother and wiped her tears. "I'm sorry I told you such things, girls," Yulana told us all. "It's alright," said Mara. "We need to know. It's better that we know."

After I had learned about what happened to Maria's aunt, I wondered if the same fate awaited Sofa's parents. I was then struck with a palpable fear that weighed on me. It made it difficult to move in the way I did before. Lines made me nervous. Going to school made me nervous. Almost everything made me nervous.

I was afraid for the safety of my parents, my siblings and myself. My little mind worked overtime trying to think of a way to overcome this uncertainty and fear. Sometimes I felt angry that I was born Jewish, but then I pushed this thought from my mind. I had made a promise to myself never to shy away from my identity. I was proud to be Jewish, but I needed to be smart as Papa said.

Then the idea came to me without much effort. Members of the communist party got preferential treatment. They were able to go jump to the front of the line for bread. They were able to buy whatever they wished. The neighbourhoods they occupied were more pleasant and secure than where the Jewish people lived.

I thought that now was the time to dedicate myself to the party. I would learn as much as I could about the communist party, and I would participate more enthusiastically and extremely than anybody else. I brought this idea to Mama, and she was confused. "I thought you hated learning about communism. Why do you want to become more involved?" I explained to Mama that I would make the friends I needed to protect us from harm. Mama laughed. "You are very sweet, but I don't think that is necessary. Papa is working on the plan with Alek to get us out of here. Soon we will go. Don't worry so much."

Mama told me not to worry, but she worried more than I did. It was impossible not to worry. The next time I saw Maria and Marta, I brought little Misha with me. He held my hand the whole time, but he was fascinated with Marta's hair. Marta picked him up and gave him some kisses. There were some moments in which we almost forgot where we were living. I treasured these moments like no other.

Maria told us that she had to leave, and I thought this was odd. Maria had just joined us. "I think you upset Yulana when you spoke about Siberia. I think Maria's mother doesn't want her around you," said Marta. I thought this was a terrible thing to say, especially if she did not know this to be absolutely true, but I made a note of Marta's comment and decided I would ask Maria the next time we spoke.

It did sound like a possibility. Maria's mother knew that I was the one who told Mark about what happened to Sofa. No matter what they said, I would understand if they did not trust me as much as they did before. Though this was completely not my fault. I tried to stop the assault from happening. It was all such a tragedy.

My first opportunity to show that I was a true comrade came quickly after my meeting with Marta. We were given an art project in which we had to draw the flag of the Ukrainian Soviet Socialist Republic. I thought this was an excellent opportunity to showcase my dedication, and make friends who could protect me, Papa, Mama and Misha. Our flag was quite simple. A red flag with the yellow state emblem, and a blue line that ran across the bottom. I was a very creative child, and despite being discouraged from playing music, I also enjoyed art. Mrs. Berdichevsky was our art teacher, and I was determined to impress her. For a couple days, I thought about how I could make my project the best in the class.

Our art supplies were limited, so we had to be creative. I decided to use the red tags we were given in the grocery store as the flag. I took a roll of them from Valarie's grocery store, and glued them together. Then I used the leftover yellow skin of a squash for the state emblem, and the blue chalk used for pool cues for the strip on the bottom. I took my time with the flag and it looked quite good.

All of the other children in class used the standard art supplies Mrs. Berdichevsky provided us with. I decided to improvise, and I thought it paid off. As one might surmise from my previous experiences with Mrs. Berdichevsky, this was not her interpretation. "How dare you defame our flag? How dare you!"

I tried to explain that I wanted to do a good job, and that it was not my intention to insult her. The reality was I spent many hours making the flag look unique, but this was precisely the problem. I was always going against the grain, even when I was finally trying to be a good comrade. The point was to blend in, and I simply could not do this. "This is disgusting. What material did you steal to make this monstrosity?" I told Mrs. Berdichevsky about the materials, and I told her why I did it, and I explained my intentions, begging for a second chance.

"A second chance? For an idiot like you?" She told me. Her voice was so irritating and high, I felt like shouting at her, but I remembered what Papa told me. They had the power. Mrs. Berdichevsky did not give me a second chance. She sent me to the principal's office yet again. I was beaten yet again, but by this time I had grown so accustomed to the belt that it the terror of the experience dulled. It was still as painful as ever, but they could no longer ruin the skin of my back. I had prominent scars that would never go away. They kept whipping me over the scar tissue.

Mrs. Berdichevsky constantly called me "stupid" and "an idiot" but she never called me a "dirty Jew" in front of the class, which I heard her say in whispers to other teachers. At least when the bums on the street tried to rob or assault me, they were direct. They would state they were doing such things because they *hated* the Jewish people. Mrs. Berdichevsky's hate was slightly more sophisticated and pernicious.

Despite all this, and the fact that she discouraged me greatly from pursuing my passion in art, and the piano teacher discouraged me so blatantly and obscenely, I knew that I was a creative person. I saw the world differently than the other girls. Nobody taught us about the concepts of justice, equality or kindness, but I knew in my heart that I longed for these things. To me, this is the essence of art. A longing to express such things. A longing to express the need for love, when it is so tragically oppressed.

Art supplies were incredibly difficult to come by. I thought I was being creative by improvising, but this was obviously not appreciated by Mrs. Berdichevsky. The piano could only be played in the home of that sadistic teacher who crushed the dreams of my sister Lena. It occurred to me then, that I had to find some other form of expression. Another form of art.

Maria was still shying away from me, and so Marta and I would get together after school. We walked to Marta's apartment building, and as we neared the apartment's front door, we heard shouting. Marta's face turned white, and she said we should probably go. "No, it's alright," I said. We entered, and Marta's mother and father were arguing over the purchase of a new television. I had never seen such a television before. It was such a rare sight. Nobody in these days had a television.

"How could you buy a television now, when your pay has been cut?" the mother shouted at the father. Marta and I were standing silently in the corner. We didn't dare interrupt them. "Well, answer me, please." The father was perhaps six feet tall. He had to bend his head to walk from room to room. "Inna, please. It's just a small luxury. I don't drink. You don't drink. Let us enjoy this television, and let Marta enjoy it too." As he said this, he noticed Marta and me in the corner.

"Children! What are you doing home at this time?" Marta told her father that it was late, and he looked at his wristwatch. "My G-d. How time flies." Marta's father was absentminded. He had difficulty paying attention.

Marta asked if we could watch television, but her father shook his head. "For now, I need to figure out how it works. Later, perhaps you can watch." The television only got three channels and all the channels were the same. It was the same as Papa's radio, so I figured we were not missing much anyway. Marta's mother scoffed and fed us some food while her father fiddled with the new television set.

I remember the tablecloth was an unusual checkered pattern. I complemented the tablecloth. "You like the tablecloth, eh? What about my cooking? Why doesn't your mother host little Marta sometimes, instead of me always having to feed you?" I thought this was rude, but I could tell Marta's mother was stressed. Sometimes people just snapped. Still, because of this I did not want to return to Marta's house. The next day at school, Marta apologized for her mother's behaviour.

I told her it was fine, and asked her if Maria's mother was still mad with me. "I don't think she's mad with you," said Marta. "I think she's afraid of what happened with Sofa. She is afraid that you could involve Maria in something similar, and she doesn't want to take any chances." This remark cut me deeply. I felt terrible about what happened to Sofa, but it wasn't my fault. I explained this to Marta. "It's not me that you have to convince," she said.

Back at the apartment, I sat on my bed and cried. Mama came to comfort me as she always did. I told her what happened with

Maria, and how her mother did not want to see me because she feared I would get Maria in trouble. Maria now avoided me at school. She would not even talk to me. "I can try to talk to her if you want," said Mama. I nodded and sobbed. I only had two close, good friends. I desperately wanted Maria back.

Mama and I traveled to Maria's house on Wihodnoy (Sunday, or the day of outing.) It was the only time we had to attend to such a matter. I was quite anxious to see Maria. She had been on my mind the whole week. When we arrived, Maria's mother did not even let us inside the house.

"What are you doing here?" she whispered at us with widened eyes. "I wanted to clear up a matter between my little Rebecca and Maria," said Mama. Maria's mother looked at me and then back at Mama. "There is nothing to discuss. Your daughter is a troublemaker. Because of her, that little girl Sofa was sent to an orphanage, and her parents were exiled. I don't want her socializing with Maria. That's the end of it." I began to cry.

I shouted that it wasn't true. Mama hushed me. "Please, there is much you don't understand. Rebecca is a good girl. I'm here to tell you the whole story," said Mama. Maria's mother would not have any of it. She slammed the door in Mama's face.

I sobbed again. Now I knew that I had lost my friend Maria.

"She's a silly woman," Mama told me as we walked back to our apartment. "She does not understand what happened. She would understand if she just listened." This was the fear that we all lived under. Misery truly did destroy the judgment of people. Maria's family was Jewish like us. We were supposed to stick together, and for her mother to treat me and Mama like that stood out forever in my mind.

I had lost two friends because of what happened with Sofa. I had lost Sofa, and I had lost Maria. Not only had I lost them, but their fathers and my father would trade services. I cried and apologized to Mama for all I had done. I could hardly walk home. We had to stop at a park bench and Mama had to console me once more.

"It's all right Rebecca, it's all right. This is not your fault. It's just an unfortunate situation." Still, I felt terrible. I was back to having only one friend, Marta.

After what had happened, I did not even have the strength to see her for a few days. I tried to be friends with non-Jews like Alla, and it turned out terribly. Then I tried to be friends with Jews, and I ended up getting them in trouble. There was no way to win. I felt trapped.

But after a few days of solitude, I needed to see Marta. We met at a spot overlooking the Dnieper River. This river is absolutely massive. It runs through Russia, Belarus and Ukraine, and it travels all the way to the Black Sea. In antiquity, it was known as the "amber road," an ancient trade route.

Nobody knew such things except for me. I was an astute little girl, and read everything I got my hands on. We watched the fishing boats travel to and from. Marta watched me carefully. Her red hair had grown wild. Usually they were kept in neat braids like mine, but she was becoming more of a rebel than I was. She put her arm over me, and gave me a hug. "I also tried to talk to Maria," she told me. "You have to know that Maria does not blame you. She wants to see you. It's just that her mother is afraid. She says hi," Marta told me. It was as though a weight were lifted off my shoulders. The fact that Maria did not blame me made me feel better.

Marta flashed me a mischievous look as we sat overlooking the river. "I discovered something," she told me. "On Wihodnoy, there is an hour of programing dedicated to children's programing. I was shocked, because my father leaves the television running all day and all night. Then on Wihodnoy, I awoke to find these strange pictures with dancing animals on television. We have to see it together. You must see it, Rebecca."

I was so excited. This was the happiest news I had heard for a long time. The next Wihodnoy, I woke up before dawn and walked to Marta's apartment. Her mother and father were sleeping, and this was for the best. We sat in front of the television which was a tiny box by today's standards. It was in her apartment that I saw my very first cartoon called "A Bag Full of Apples."

I was mesmerized by a talking and singing bunny rabbit. The story was so moving and emotional. I observed with great care the varied voices of the characters, and the wonderful artwork that was hand drawn at the time. The music was also fantastic. It was about a little bunny rabbit who traveled through the forest to collect apples for his family. Along the way he gave away an apple here and an apple there to his forest friends.

Then a nasty crow tore a hole in his bag, and the rabbit had to return to the apple tree. It was there where he encountered a wolf who chased him all the way home. When he arrived home, he cried to his family that he had laboured all day without anything to show for it. But as is the case in most cartoons, he did not need to worry for long.

The friends that he helped in the forest ended up returning the favour, and his family ate well and did not need to worry about food. The bear to whom he gave apples, gave his family honey to return the favour. The mole he gave apples to, gave his family vegetables, and so on.

"The bunny was too gullible to listen to the crow," said Marta. "No," I said. "The point of the story is that if you are generous you will be rewarded." Marta thought about it and agreed with me. "Well that's nice, but it's not real life," she said. I agreed with Marta, it was not realistic. But I did not think art needed to be realistic. Even at this young age, I grasped this concept. Art was supposed to be what we could imagine.

I never threw away the flag Mrs. Berdichevsky criticized so harshly. I thought it was a symbol of my rebellion. Cartoons were yet another artistic medium that was unavailable to me, but I thought about ideas for cartoons. I thought a lot about kindness during this time. For reasons, I could not quite put my finger on, I knew that what was going on around me was not right.

I felt deep in my soul that this wickedness should be alleviated. This wickedness needed to be changed to kindness. How did I know this? Perhaps it was just my nature. But seeing this cartoon confirmed what I felt. Despite all I had lost, and all that I had been subjected to, the injustice and the cruelty, I knew there was another way. I was grateful to have Marta as a friend. At least I had one friend. It kept me going during these most trying times.

Chapter Seven

White Lies & Black Caviar

One evening I came home from school to find Papa next to the radio talking with Alek. Alek greeted me with a warm and familiar smile. We ate dinner together, and I helped Mama prepare soup and salad. Alek and my father looked more tired than usual. During this time of economic stagnation, our parents would work harder and harder, only to be compensated less and less.

The price of bread was rising almost every week, while wages stayed the same. There was a sense of urgency in the air. We had to get out of this place, and as time went on, Papa and Alek talked in secret during the night more frequently. Now he was over for dinner, and I wondered why. We had been incredibly careful around our neighbours, and this was a significant risk to have visitors. It raised suspicion.

It was *Shabbat*. Just a few months ago we were able to have Grandma Yael and Grandpa Elie over, but now it was too dangerous. Our neighbours were always watching us, and in the apartment, you could hear voices through the wall if you listened closely. If we were interrogated, we would simply say he was a dinner guest, but luckily, we had only had one previous encounter when the KGB barged into our apartment, and this was an accident. We were not on the radar. Not yet, at least.

Alek was such a dignified presence. He ate and spoke with utmost respect and politeness towards others, a stark contrast to many adults I had encountered outside our home. As we ate, he asked me about school. I told him that I could not stand it, and then Mama scolded me. "Please do not complain so much," she asked. I felt bad for complaining, but it seemed that Alek was one of the few adults that would understand.

After dinner, I helped Mama clean the kitchen, and I fed Misha. He was growing bigger every day, and despite the tiny portions we fed him, he looked healthy and strong. I thanked G-d that Misha was doing all right. One had to remember to be thankful in this time too. This was another lesson I learned very early on. The importance of gratitude.

Papa and Alek spoke softly again in front of the radio. Papa became aware of his nervous habits and tried to get rid of them. When he would become nervous, he would sketch something on his drafting paper, and so he did this while he spoke with Alek. Then something quite surprising happened. They called me over to speak with them. Papa asked me to sit down in his chair, and they stood over me.

Papa hovered over me, hiding what appeared to be a concerned look in his eyes. Alek's demeanour was unchanged. Alek considered me carefully, with eyes that felt as though they were looking directly through me. "Rebecca, your father tells me that you have struggled keeping some friends at school," said Alek. "Yes, but it wasn't my fault. I want to tell you what happened," I said. Alek raised his finger to his thin lips, signalling to me that there was no need to explain.

"It's okay. I don't need to know about such things. I know you are a good girl, and it was not your fault. I had an idea, well, a connection really, with a family I know. They have two lovely daughters about your age, and I thought it might be nice if you were to meet them."

This idea made me incredibly excited. I was such an extroverted child, and I loved Marta like a sister, but I was incredibly pleased with the prospect of meeting more girls around my age. I said yes immediately, and Alek laughed. "See, that wasn't too hard," he told my father. My father grimaced. "What's the matter Papa?" I asked. "Nothing my little Regoletta. I'm just tired from work."

Alek and my father sat for a while and talked about this and that, and then he left. The next little while was uneventful. I spoke with Marta, went to school, and tended to all of my usual chores. Life became more arduous when it came to everyday tasks. The hatred of our people increased. But this was nothing new.

The next memorable event was when Alek made his appearance in front of my parent's apartment building. Now he was driving a bright red ZAZ passenger car. It was exceptionally rare to own a car. This was a luxury few people could say they had, and it was the first time I ever even rode in a car. The ZAZ factory was founded in 1923 and the first ZAZ-965 resembled an even smaller version of today's Mini Cooper. They were truly tiny on the inside, and Alek was quite skilled at driving it. He shifted effortlessly from gear to gear. I was extremely impressed.

"How does it feel to ride in a ZAZ? It's a pretty fun car, don't you think Rebecca?" I was holding onto the door, because Alek was driving so quickly through the narrow streets. Every time he cornered it felt as though we were going to tip over. "This is so much fun!" I shouted over the noise of the engine.

We drove for quite a while until we arrived in a neighbourhood I had never seen before. I was only familiar with the streets around my first apartment, and our second apartment where we now lived. The streets here were different. They were clean, and the people seemed more civilized. There were hardly any beggars or drunks in the street. The apartment buildings also looked better maintained than where we lived.

We sat in the car and Alek played nervously with a sliver plated lighter he took out of his breast pocket. He did not smoke, but he kept a lighter for friends who did. "Remember I told you about my friend with the two daughters I wanted you to meet?" asked Alek. "Of course," I said. Alek cleared his throat and pointed to a house across the street from where we were parked. "Well, he's not actually my friend. This man is a *friend of a friend* of mine. He does not know me. His name is Alexey and he has two daughters. Both of his daughters are about your age. Olya and Nika."

I thought this was strange. Why would Alek take me to someone who he did not know? He continued: "Now, his daughters play on this street every day after school at about six. You can meet them and play with them. Maybe become friends with them. But I need you to promise me one thing."

"Okay," I said. "You cannot tell Olya or Nika or Alexey about me. You also cannot tell them that you know me, or the fact that you are Jewish."

"Why would I lie about those things?" I asked Alek. "It's not really a lie. It is a white lie. A little lie, that you would tell if the subject ever came up. Introduce yourself by the *goyish* name your mother gave you." This made me quite upset. "I hate that name," I told Alek. "Well you can name yourself anything you want," he told me.

I thought about it, but I did not like what Alek was telling me. I wanted to tell them my real name, and wondered what was really going on here. I wondered why there were all these secrets and why Alek waited to tell me all this now, when he could have told me in front of Papa, back home. "I don't want to hide the fact that I'm Jewish," I told Alek. "And also, I don't know why you did not tell me all this when we were with Papa."

Alek laughed. "You are too smart for your own good, Rebecca. Now, I understand everything you said. And, you are right. So, let me be honest with you now. Your father and I are planning something. For your own safety, you cannot know why or how. The important thing is, by being friends with these girls, you will be helping us. Become friends with them, and just worry about that for now. Once you become friends, then I will need to know some more information. This will be helpful to me, and to your father. It will be helpful to our effort to leave the Soviet Union. That is as much as I can tell you now. Soon I will tell you more. But you must promise me one thing," said Alek.

Alek was profoundly serious now, as he grabbed my arm and gripped it so hard that the skin turned white. "You cannot repeat any of what I told you to those girls or their father. Your task is to become friends with them, and conceal the fact that you are Jewish. Do you understand?"

"Yes, I do," I said.

I could not believe what I was hearing, and I wanted to know why. Alek reached over me and opened the passenger door of the car. The car was so small, he could do this quite easily. "I will park here in two hours to pick you up. If they ask you where you are from, or who your parents are, lie to them. Tell them anything you want, but do not reveal your true identity."

With that, Alek drove away, and I was on a street I had never seen before, surrounded by unfamiliar people and unfamiliar stores. There were still line ups, but everything seemed calmer here. The people appeared to be more relaxed than were I was from. I walked to where the home was, and I waited for a while. Just as Alek said, at around six, the two girls left their home, and began playing hopscotch on the street.

Olya wore round wire glasses and had platinum blonde hair. She was a pretty girl and she was very thin. Her sister Nika was quite the opposite. She had darker hair and she was quite plump. I wondered how these two girls could be sisters. They saw me almost immediately and invited me to join. There were hardly any other children on the street. The neighbourhood was completely different from my parents. There were also many more cars here. I saw some government vehicles parked in front of the houses. This usually meant that they were part of the faction of the KGB.

Olya told me where she and Nika went to school, and asked if I went there. I told her that I did not, but then I remembered I was not supposed to tell them anything about myself. I made up a "white lie" that I just moved here from Moscow. "What is Moscow like?" asked Nika. I panicked when she asked me this. It was fun to make up lies, but not so fun when you had to remember them. The story I heard before about the bananas came to mind, and so I just repeated that story to Nika.

"There are many bananas there," I told Nika. "There are lines at the stores, just like there are here, but party members get to go first, and they have an abundance of bananas, which are a yellow fruit that are very delicious."

"I know what bananas are," said Nika.

"Yeah," said Olya. "Don't you have bananas at home?" This caught me off guard. "Yes, of course. I just thought you might not have known about Moscow, and how popular bananas are over there."

We played hopscotch for quite some time, and then Olya and Nika got tired. We all sat outside, and Alexey called the girls to come inside. Alexey was a burly man. He did not seem friendly, and I do not think he even noticed I was playing with his girls. "Maybe see you again," said Olya. "You tell funny stories, Alice," said Nika. "Thank you, yes, let's play again," I said. I gave myself the name of Alice.

I returned to the street where Alek picked me up, and I saw his red car pull around the corner. We sped away back to my parent's apartment. "How did it go?" he asked me. "It was good. I played hopscotch with them," I said. Alek swore very loudly. He slammed the horn with his fist. A truck traveling in the opposite direction swerved into oncoming traffic and nearly hit us. There were crazy and drunk drivers everywhere. The driving was nothing like it was in Canada, where everyone obeyed the traffic laws.

If the light were red, people would ignore the signal and drive through. There were lots of injuries and death from driving accidents, and now I was beginning to become a little frightened, driving with Alek.

"Did they invite you inside?" Alek asked me. "No, they didn't," I said. "Next time you should try to be invited inside. What I need you to do is memorize the apartment. If there are any documents or items belonging to their father, Alexey, I need you to memorize them and tell me about them. Word for word."

Now I was curious as to what my real mission was. I asked Alek, but he said he still could not tell me. "I will tell you after you collect this information," he told me. The sky turned into wonderful shades of violet and crimson hues as we drove home. It settled into a dark shade of violet and blue as we arrived at my parent's apartment.

Mama was worried sick, but Papa knew where I was. This caused an argument. "I demand to know what is going on this instant," said Mama. "Alek needs Rebecca to help him for work," said Papa. He was fiddling with the refrigerator to avoid talking with Mama. It sounded like it was going to break again, except now there was no one to fix it.

Mama did not give up. "Why can't you tell me what's going on?" she asked my father. Papa put down his tools and looked at Mama and then at me. "Alek said Rebecca is safe. She just needs to help Alek with some administrative work," he said winking at me.

"Rebecca, is this true?"

"Yes, Mama," I said. Shortly after this argument, I went out for a walk with Papa. "I don't understand all of these secrets, Papa," I said. "What exactly does Alek want me to do?" Papa looked worried again. He put his finger to his mouth. "We are not supposed to talk about such things. People can hear us," he said.

We walked for another block and then Papa looked both ways to see if anybody was listening. Then he knelt to speak with me. "Alek told me that you are working on something especially important. He assured me that you will be safe, and I trust that man with my life. He saved my life back in the war. Do what he says, and don't ask too many questions," Papa told me.

I was frustrated that Papa did not even ask me what I was doing. I could have been prostituted for all he knew, but he did not ask me, and I felt hurt. Still, that night was one of the most exciting of my entire life. I felt like a secret agent. How could I pay attention at school after an event like that?

The teachers ridiculed and beat me as usual, but I still had Marta as a real friend I could rely on. Now our time together was extremely limited, but I clung to her, and I told myself that our relationship was real. I did not have the heart to lose another friend. Not after what happened with Alex, Sofa and then Maria. I decided to keep my secret from Marta, for now.

Alek picked me up a few days later and we preformed the same routine. Eventually Olya felt comfortable enough to ask me to come over for dinner. I told her that I would next time. I did not want to say yes before asking Alek.

When I told Alek this on the car ride back, I could sense that he was upset with me. He was upset that I said no. He wished I would have said yes immediately. Alek had never been upset with me. "I'm not mad at you," he reassured me. "It's just that this is taking longer than I anticipated." He played with his sliver lighter, flicking the top off and then clicking it back on again. Then he snapped his fingers.

"You know something," he told me. "I think it's actually better that we have time to plan. I want you in that house long enough so that you can find as much information as possible. You need to ask to sleepover at their place. Go to Olya, tell her that your mother and father are fighting, and cry a lot so that they offer for you to sleep over. If they do not offer, then say you are too afraid to go home and ask them." I had only known these girls for two weeks, and I did not think that would work, but I told Alek I would give it a try.

"What do I tell them about my parents? I don't think I can remember all these lies," I said. "Try not to give them names. Try not to give any information you do not have to. The less you say, the less you must remember later. But if they insist, use the parents of one of your friends, that way it will be easier to remember," said Alek.

I was now quite frightened, and I told Alek I had to tell Mama and Papa that I would be gone for the night, something I have never done before. We were driving in circles, but now we finally arrived at our usual spot. Alek pulled the parking brake up and pat me on the top of the head.

"I will tell your parents that you are with me. Do not worry about that. All you need to do is stay the night, and memorize everything in the house. Go through Alexey's desk drawers. Go through anything you think belongs to him. Put everything back the way you found it, but remember everything. Okay?"

"Yes, Alek," I said.

When the day came to do what we had planned, my heart was beating out of my chest. I thought of everything the teachers at school had put me through. I thought of Alex and Sofa, my sister, the piano teacher, how my Mama was treated, and all of the suffering and pain inside my heart. Almost immediately I burst into tears and it kept coming and coming.

I did not have to venture far from where Alek dropped me off. Olya and Nika came running towards me. "What's wrong Alice? Why are you crying?" I told them that my parents got into a terrible fight and my Papa hurt my Mama. I told them he threw a bottle against her face and her eye was cut. I told them I did not want to come home. Olya gave me a hug. "It's all right. Let me ask my dad if you can sleep over tonight, so you don't have to go home." I was astonished at how easy our plan worked. It was almost too good to be true.

Olya and Nika led me back to the house where their father Alexey had yet to arrive home from work. The mother, whom I never met, was home cooking some vegetable soup for dinner. I can still remember the smell of this soup. It was different from Jewish cooking. They used different spices and they mixed meat and dairy. I was worried that they would serve me both at the same time, but luckily there was only soup for dinner.

The mother lounged on a sofa with a fabric made from wonderfully intricate patterns. She was quite beautiful, but far too pale. Her crimson lipstick contrasted her pale complexion, and her eyes had dark bags underneath them, despite an abundance of makeup.

"Who is this child?" she asked Olya. Olya bowed her head in a way that suggested she was afraid of her mother. "Our friend Alice. She had a dreadful day, Mama. Can she sleep over tonight?"

The mother looked at me with disinterest. "Do not touch anything. We have wonderful things in this house, young lady," she told me. "Yes," I said softly. My eyes were still red with tears. I found the mother to be interesting to observe. She was melancholy and she moved slowly. I wondered if she was suspicious of me. There were flags everywhere inside the house. This was the house of a communist party member. The first I had ever seen. The furniture was nicer than ours, but by no means fancy.

Soon afterwards, Alexey, Olya and Nika's father, arrived home. He was dressed in uniform. Alexey was KGB. At this time, I still knew little about the party. I knew what they taught me in school, but nothing else. Alexey had a hat with the emblem of the KGB placed in the center. He put his hat by the door, and called to his wife.

"Dinner is ready," said Olya's mother. "Why must you be so melancholy all the time? Why are you never happy to see me?" Alexey asked his wife. Then Alexey saw me and quickly realized that there was one too many children in his home. "Who is this little girl?" He said this as though I were a piece of furniture. He was quite intimating. His voice was booming, and he looked to be physically very strong. He held an exceptionally large, domineering presence. "One of the children's friends from school," said Olya's mother. "Oh," said Alexey.

We all sat down for dinner and the family said grace. They were Christians. I did not know the prayer. When they asked me to say it with them, I apologized and said I was too upset, but that I would pray silently. Then the meal began. It was simply bread and soup. I could tell Olya and Nika's parents were not interested in hearing from the children. It was not common for children to be involved in discussion with adults. The Jewish people were different. They enjoyed intellectual conversations. They encouraged it for their children. It was true children sat at separate tables, but their voice was still valued.

The Passover holiday has a portion in which there is a conscious effort to educate the children. This part of the "*seder*" is called the four questions. The *goyish* population were different. Children were to be seen and not heard at all. This was indeed preferable for my purposes.

Olya, Nika and I sipped our soup silently, while Alexey and his wife spoke. "They are thinking of transferring me," said Alexey. He took a big spoonful of soup and slurped it very loudly. His wife sighed. "Oh yes? To where?" she asked. Alexey eyes flashed with rage. I could tell he did not care for his wife in the way my Papa cared for Mama. There was a coldness between them.

"They are thinking of moving me to Moscow to work as a translator. But I like what I am doing now. I enjoy tracking down the dissenters, the nationalists, and the anti-Soviet scum. I don't know what will happen."

The wife was unmoved by her husband's big news. I would have thought she would be excited or frightened, or any other kind of emotion other than disinterested, but it seemed she did not care. "Did you hear what I just said, woman?" asked Alexey, rudely. Alexey's wife nodded ever so slowly. "Yes, darling. I heard. I do not care one way or the other. What difference does it make?"

Alexey slammed the table so that everything shook. The soup bowl tipped over and the thick vegetable puree oozed everywhere. "Dammit you stupid woman! I like my post. I like tracking down those disgusting Jews and nationalists and making them pay. If I am transferred, that means we are all transferred. That means our entire life will change. What is wrong with you?"

The wife sighed and told Olya and Nika to clean up the soup that had spilled. "You are right, darling. You are always right," said Alexey's wife in the same tone. I could tell this answer only served to infuriate Alexey further.

He wanted his wife to care. He wanted her to become angry or happy or frightened, but she did not. It was clear that she did not care. I thought it was brave, what she did. She could have pretended, but instead she defied him, in her own way. The tension at the table was palpable, and I was frightened just to be in the room with them. I was on edge. I do not know how these girls lived in this home without going crazy. Perhaps that was one of the reasons they were always outside, playing.

Alexey gripped his spoon so hard that he bent the handle, but then he looked over at his two daughters, and composed himself. "Olya, clean the soup. Nika, bring me my pipe," he commanded. "Yes father," the girls said in unison. Then it was only me and Alexey at the table. If I had not been so young at the time, I don't think I could have repeated this act. I was frightened, yes. But I did not understand the gravity of my situation. Crossing the KGB ends in imprisonment or death if they found out, and if you were a Jew, the punishment was no doubt harsher than anyone else.

The main functions of the KGB were foreign intelligence, counter-intelligence, operative-investigatory activities, guarding the state border of the USSR; guarding the leadership of the Central Committee of the Communist Party, the Central Committee of the Communist party, the Soviet Government, the organization and security of government communications, and finally combating nationalism, dissent and anti-Soviet activities. Alexey was an agent who was dedicated to fighting dissent. He was a dedicated agent, a fact which I would soon discover.

I was sitting with an agent whose job it was to imprison or kill Jewish people like me. A little girl and a grown man. He had no idea who I was, why I was there, or what I was about to do. To be honest, I did not know why I was there either, but I had a foggy idea. I knew that Alek needed information, and I sat in silence while Alexey looked at me with an irritated expression on his face.

"So, you are school friends with Olya and Nika?" He asked me. "Yes, we play hopscotch together," I said. "That's fine. I think you should go home now. It's getting late," said Alexey. I did not know what to say. I did not want to disagree with him or say no. Luckily Nika came to my rescue. She placed Alexey's pipe on the table. It was filled with sweet tobacco. Alexey lit the pipe and I could see he felt a little more relaxed.

"Father, Alice had a distressing day. Her parents got into a tiff. We asked Mother if she could sleep over," said Nika. Alexey grunted. He looked at me, then he looked at Nika. "Fine, what do I care?" he muddled. Then he told Nika and Olya to get away from him. As soon as Olya finished cleaning up the spilled soup and put away the dishes, we all went back to Olya and Nika's bedroom.

Along the way I made note of everything in the house. Alexey's hat and wallet were placed on a little glass table in the narrow hallway that led to the two bedrooms in the house. Olya and Nika's bedroom had nothing of interest inside, although they did have a record player, which I was very fascinated by. They had a vinyl record of the Beatles, and I asked them to play it, but they said that they couldn't at this hour, and that their father would go into a rage if he heard it. Olya told us that we had to keep our voices down.

"I'm just glad Father does not hit Mother like your parents do," Nika said to me. I thought this was extremely rude, even though my whole story was a farce. Olya immediately corrected her. "That's not nice to say," said Olya. "I'm sorry I didn't mean it," said Nika. I told Nika that I forgave her and then it was time for bed. Olya gave me a blanket to sleep with on the floor. I slept on the floor in between Olya and Nika, and I felt bad that that I was lying to them. Even thought they were not Jewish, I thought they would make good friends. Then I thought about how Alla was a good friend, until she told on me. It was so rare to encounter a genuinely good person in this world.

The house did not take long to fall silent. I was wide awake but Olya and Nika were sleeping. I had to carefully open the door to their room without alerting them. I did this and then saw that the light to their parents' bedroom across the hall was dark. Alexey and his wife were asleep too.

Every step I took was delicate and deliberate. I made sure to balance my weight so that I made as little noise as possible. This was not very difficult as I was not very heavy. The apartment was almost pitch dark, and I wondered how I would be able to navigate it. Just then the streetlight from outside flickered to light. There was a dim shadow which provided just enough light for me to see.

I went straight to Alexey's wallet and hat located on the glass table. The wallet did not look like anything unusual. I examined it. It had his identification card and party member card with his face on it. I memorized his ID number, but I did not think any of the other information was important.

Next, I searched the drawers of Alexey's desk. There was a black book with names and numbers inside. I saw ten names and ten numbers. Alek told me to memorize everything but there was too much information to memorize. I remembered my sister Lena practicing a sonata by Chopin. I tried to create a song to remember all the names and numbers, but after ten minutes of whispering to myself, I could not remember. The stress of the situation was too high. I was too nervous about being caught.

So, I frantically searched for a pen on Alexey's desk and a scrap of paper. By the dim light of the mood I copied the names and numbers, and put everything back the way I found it, like Alek said to do.

I thought I was certainly time to get back to my friend's room at this point, so I tip-toed back and snuck under the blanket Olya had given me. I was astonished to find them both sleeping quite heavily. Nobody noticed what I had done. I just had to get out of there with that scrap of paper.

In the morning, Alexey and his wife were in the kitchen speaking about something. His wife was eating black caviar, a delicacy that I had never seen before. As Olya, Nika, and I entered the kitchen she offered us some. "Don't feed them that! Don't you know how expensive it is?" Alexey shouted at his wife.

"They can have mine, darling," she said without any inflection in her voice. It looked as though she had slept in her makeup from the day before. "Here children, taste a little on a cracker. Enjoy. Otherwise, what is the point? You have to enjoy yourself while you are alive, because the good times are short, and then you die, and there is nothing."

She scraped her caviar onto a plate and offered us each a cracker. I tasted this strange food, and tried to keep from heaving it up. It was crunchy and far too salty. Olya and Nika seemed to have the same reaction as I did. Alexey kicked one of the kitchen chairs and the chair went flying.

"That's the most expensive caviar from the Black Sea. It was given to me as a gift from my boss, and you fed it to the bloody children! Something is wrong with your brain, woman. Something is not right with you."

They started arguing, and I left with Olya and Nika. They were going to school, but I was not going with them. "When will you start to go to school with us?" asked Olya. "I'm not sure, but soon," I said. "Okay, well, see you later. I hope everything at your parents' house is okay."

"Thank you," I said.

I waited for Alek at our usual spot. He arrived in the red car and we were off. "I got some names and numbers Alexey had in his desk. I wrote them down, because I could not remember them," I said. Alek's face turned white. "Did they notice anything?" "No," I said. "They got into an argument. I don't think they noticed."

Alek turned the corner and we parked in a gas station. "Let me see the list," he said. He looked them over and shook his head. "All right, this is good. This is incredibly good. I will find out who these people are. Now that you are safe, I can tell you the plan. But we must drive. We must not sit here like this."

We were off again, driving through the city streets towards the direction of my school. It was going to be a close race to get me to school on time. If I was late, I would surely get a beating from the principal, but I didn't care. Alek began to tell me why I just did what I did:

"Your father and I are part of a large operation. It is one of the largest operations intended to get the Jewish community out from here, and to the land of Israel. In order to do this, we need particular documents."

"Now, most of these documents are not easy or even possible to get without bribes. If we need to bribe party officials, we will do this, with the help of our friends from the Jewish community in New York City and in Canada. However, there are some officials that will not take bribes. They will not 'dirty their hands' by dealing with Jews. That is what you are helping me with. Agent Alexey is part of a special task force designed to snuff out dissenters."

"He will not take a bribe to look the other way. In fact, he is so loyal, that he would turn against his own agents if it meant imprisoning or killing a Jew. The problem, is we need agent Alexey to look the other way."

Alexey, I was told, was investigating a party official, who we bribed to give us a substantial number of health certificates. Alexey will not take a bribe, so we needed to find some information on him that would force him to look the other way without one.

I recognized the streets again. The time was nearly 8:30 AM and school was about to begin. Alek put his foot on the gas so that we could make it on time. "Now," continued Alek, "as I said, if Alexey will not take a bribe. That is why I asked you to become friends with his daughters."

What Alek was saying made sense, but I was not sure how the little piece of information I received would be helpful. It was a crazy thing to do what I had done, and if Mama knew, or if Papa knew the full extent of my activities, my feeling was that they would not be pleased with Alek. Still, it was incredibly exciting, and I wondered what my next task would be.

We arrived at my school. The time was 8:40 AM and I was late, but I didn't care. "When will I see you again, Alek?" I asked. "Soon," he told me. "I have business to discuss with your father. Now be good at school, and do not listen to what they tell you. You are an incredibly special girl, and you are very smart." Hearing him say that made me feel very good. I wanted to tell Alek everything that they did to me. I did not want to leave the car. "Go on," he said, "do what you need to do." I went to school and I received the belt yet again for being late.

Chapter Eight

A Microphone Behind The Mirror

I was in the hospital beside Mama, and I was crying so violently that I shook. Papa was massaging my neck. He was telling me it was going to be okay, and that Mama would recover. Alek was nowhere to be found. I wished Alek was there with us. I was holding Misha and he was fidgeting in my arms, but he could also sense something was not right. He knew something was seriously wrong with Mama, and we all cried.

All the time I spent with Alek meant that there was no one to do the grocery shopping. As a result, Mama went to the grocer and was again refused service because she was Jewish. Valarie was not working. It was an employee of his who was deeply anti-semitic. When Mama came to the front of the line, he mocked her nose.

"He told me it looked like I was a toucan from the jungle. That is what he told me. What a horrible thing he said to me in front of all those people. And the worst part was everyone in line laughed at me," said Mama.

After the grocer had mocked Mama, a man in line went into a rage and asked why he had to stand behind a Jew.

When nobody answered him, he left his spot in line, grabbed Mama, and threw her down onto the street. Nobody left the line to help her. Eventually, a passerby did help her and called an ambulance, but everyone in line laughed at Mama as she bled on the sidewalk. Things were becoming worse. The hatred towards Jews was deepening.

The doctor walked in and politely told Mama to stop crying because it would ruin the bandages around her nose and cheeks. He was a tall, thin man with dark hair and an extremely low, soft voice and an unusual name. I was not sure where he was from.

"You have a concussion and a broken nose. This will take some time to heal, and you need to rest in bed," said the doctor. "The danger with concussion is that if you don't rest, you can have swelling, and this can cause it to become worse," he said quickly. The doctor mumbled. It was difficult to hear him. "I am going to have you stay one more night in hospital, and then I will send you home with pain medications. But for now, I am going to give you more morphine," said the doctor. Then he left.

When my sister Lena heard about what happened to Mama, she also came to the hospital. Her husband did not show up. I was suspicious as to why. She looked tired and thin. I wondered how her new husband was treating her, but I did not dare to ask. I was just happy to see her. She gave me a warm hug, and we all sat outside Mama's room. Papa paced up and down the hospital hallway. "Well, she is sleeping here for the night. Let us go back home and get some rest. Then we will come back for her in the morning. Lena, can you please stay with us for the night?"

"Of course, I can," said my sister. We all walked home. I carried Misha and it felt a little like old times when everyone was home.

Except, there was one major difference. Mama was missing. It was not the same at all without Mama there. The house felt empty without her.

I did my best to cook dinner for everyone, but the task was great. I had to feed Papa, Misha, myself and Lena. Mama usually handled the stove, and I tried to light the stove, but it wasn't working. I got frustrated and kicked it. "Hey! Do not damage the stove. We need at least one appliance to work right around here," said Papa quite sternly. This made me terribly upset, and I served dinner, but it was not the same as when Mama did it. Lena could tell I was upset.

After dinner, Lena told me she had a surprise for me. I asked her what it was, and she told me to go to the bathroom. She produced a black case with a zipper. Inside the case was lipstick, mascara, and various other makeup.

I had never worn makeup before. It was rare to see women wearing makeup. Lena smiled at me and took out some blush. "My husband was able to get it, because of someone he knows who works for the ballet. It is fine quality. I know you are a little young for makeup, but I thought it might be fun."

"Oh yes," I said. "I want to see how it looks." I wanted to look like a ballerina. The mirror to the bathroom hung above the sink. As Lena painted my face with a pink blush, we both looked into the mirror. Then, Lena stopped. Her eyes grew wide, and she focused her gaze at the bottom right corner of the mirror. There was a piece of the wall, next to the mirror that was chipped. Lena put her finger over her mouth to signal to me to be quiet.

She gently lifted the mirror towards us. Behind the mirror was a microphone, and the wire to the microphone went through the wall into the next apartment. Lena gently placed the mirror back and told me that my makeup made me look very pretty. We both made gestures to Papa to turn off his radio and hide it. Then we whispered quietly that we all needed to talk outside.

Lena, Papa and I took a long walk and made sure nobody could hear us. We were walking through a park. Then Lena told Papa the news. "Do you know how long that microphone has been there?" she asked. Papa rubbed the stubble on his face. "I have no clue. It could be days or months. I wonder if it could hear my radio. I don't think it can because I listen to it on a low volume. I should call Alek and see what can be done about this situation."

It was common for the KGB to pay neighbours to spy on each other, especially if they knew or suspected the neighbours to be Jewish. It was good that Lena discovered the bug, but it was frightening that we did not know for how long the bug was planted.

The next day was quite busy. Mama had to be picked up from the hospital. Alek picked Mama and Papa up from the hospital, and then arrived home in the morning. I did not have many belongings. A change of clothing and my childhood stuffed animal was all that I had. My parents gathered all their important documents, the radio and a few appliances. Everything had to fit in Alek's tiny car and there was barely enough room for four people, let alone four people plus my brother Misha and all our belongings. "Whatever doesn't fit, I will come back for," said Alek.

We began the drive to the cottage, and the car was extremely uncomfortable to sit in. I held Misha on my lap, and there were no seatbelts at this time, so the driving was very unsafe. When Alek drove, we all closed our eyes and prayed we would arrive to our destination without crashing. "It does not matter what the neighbour heard or did not hear. It is not safe for you to live in that apartment anymore. The city is becoming more and more dangerous for Jews," Said Alek.

My father sat in the front seat with Alek and turned around to check on us. "We are fine, dear," my mother smiled. She was still in a lot of pain, and she should not have been traveling like this with a concussion. Still, she did not complain. In fact, I might have actually seen a little smile on her face. We were finally getting out of the city. The country life was so much better.

Then my heart sank when I remembered I never said goodbye to Marta. It had been a long time since I had seen her. I wondered if I would be allowed to contact her again, but Alek said it was far too dangerous to do so. I had lost yet another friend because of this senseless hatred. It was most depressing.

When we arrived at our *dacha* we discovered everything was as we left it. This was a most welcome surprise. We expected the place to be trashed or looted. Alek had arranged the paperwork for us to travel north to our *dacha*. When Mama tried to exit the car, she threw up due to her concussion. We made sure to lie her down and give her some water which I fetched from the same well as before.

When the night came, it was time for Alek and Papa to speak. We lit a fire and they ate some whitefish that we all had a part in making. I listened to them, as I slept in my bunk with Misha. "I will find someone who will rent your apartment, and I will be sure to set you up somewhere else in the city so that you may continue to work. Don't worry," Alek said to Papa.

Papa left all his shaving gear at home, and so he had a five o'clock shadow that was already growing. "What happened with the health certificates?" asked Papa. Alek laughed aloud. Then he covered his mouth, remembering there were sleeping in the house.

"Let me tell you something, Vladimir. Your daughter saved us. That list she brought me. It turned out that the names on that list were the names and numbers of Alexey's lovers, and not all of them were women. He is homosexual." I did not see Papa's jaw drop, but I could have imagined it dropping. "What? Really? That is so illegal! Jail or even worse – death for him! But why is this important?" said Papa. "Well," said Alek, "his wife may not care one way or another. But I found someone in the KGB who I will pay to tell Alexey that we know he is a homosexual, and we will expose him to the rest of the office if he does not allow comrade Bogdan to issue health certificates for the influx of Jewish applications to leave the Union. I think this plan is good. I think he will cave in and allow the certificates to be issued."

The plan to obtain the health certificates was only one barrier to leave the Soviet Union. There were many other certificates and paperwork that had to be obtained for the Jewish population to leave. We were, however, making significant progress, and Alek told my father this.

The plan was for us to move in with Papa's family. They lived in a neighbourhood that was now safer to live in. The neighbours did not spy as much. Initially, we invited them to our apartment for *Shabbat*, because theirs was too dangerous. Now the situation was reversed. Papa and Alek decided we would stay one day at the *dacha* and then we would move in with my father's parents.

My task was the same as before at the *dacha*, to fetch water, and do some light chores. Only now Mama was incapacitated, so I had more responsibilities. Between this time and the time we left the country, I would develop a passion and skill for cooking. I had to be creative. We never had all the necessary ingredients. I would not measure exactly; I would feel and experiment with different flavors. Sometimes this was a good thing, and Papa liked it, and sometimes it was not so good. Papa always told me when he did not like the food I prepared. But I learned this was okay, because it meant I would learn how to do it better the next time.

I did not want to go back to school. I wanted to stay at our *dacha*, although the weather was not the nicest now. It was winter, and the rooms were cold at night. Alek and Papa sat by the fire, and spoke through the night. I always wanted to know more of what they were up to. I would have never dreamed that I would be a part of the operation. My small role helped Papa and Alek with the health certificates, and I was quite proud I was able to help. I wondered if they would need me again.

When we moved back to the city, I got to spend a lot more time with my grandparents. I got to know them well, and they taught me more about what it meant to be Jewish. My father's grandfather was a rabbi and so my grandparents were deeply knowledgeable and religious.

We were extra careful about the neighbours now. Luckily, they did not seem interested in our business. We had two neighbours, as we were on a corner unit. In the apartment, next to us, there lived an elderly couple. Across the hall there was a young family. The new apartment was very tight. There was Papa, Mama, me, Misha and Papa's parents, Elie and Yael. There was also no refrigerator, so Papa did not have to worry about repairing it anymore.

CHAPTER NINE

Wisdom from My Elders

MY GRANDFATHER ELIE WORE SPECTACLES, and had an exceptionally long salt and pepper beard. He was incredibly wise, and he enjoyed giving me lectures that his father passed down to him. Papa had already heard of these lessons, of course. But Papa was not as interested in learning about what it meant to be a Jew like I did.

I was always upset that I never had a *bat-mitzvah* (the girl's version of *bar-mitzvah*). When boys reach the age of thirteen, they study the Torah and read a portion in the synagogue. This is an ancient tradition which marks the point at which a Jewish boy becomes a man.

Mama eventually recovered from her injuries, and we shared the kitchen work again. After dinner, I would go to Grandfather Elie and he would give me a lecture. Mama was pleased, but also frightened. We were aware of the neighbours now, and she cautioned us to always be quiet.

My grandfather had a magnificent laugh. It was almost like a cackle that sounded like a crow, but it was a welcoming, soft cackle. He asked me why I thought Christians often say that Christianity is a religion that preaches love, while Judaism is regarded by Christians as stern and legalistic.

I told him I had no idea. My grandfather said that the Christians like to point to verses like Matthew 5:43-44: You have heard that it was said, 'Love your neighbour and hate your enemy.' But I tell you, love your enemies and pray for those who persecute you.

But he said they twist the interpretation. He explained that the Proverbs say, "let not your heart be glad when your enemy falls, lest the Lord see it and it displeases Him."

I needed to ask my grandfather to slow down, and explain what that meant and was patient with me. He was far more patient than any of my teachers. My grandfather knew so much about Judaism, and every day after school he would tell me a little bit of knowledge.

My grandmother Yael was an excellent cook, but she had moods and night terrors from the concentration camp. It was strange how the Holocaust traumatized some people irreversibly, while other people seemed to be able to block out the trauma. I always wondered why Papa and grandfather Elie could never talk about it, while my grandmother Yael and Alek could.

Grandma Yael would scream in her sleep and wake everyone up, but after her night terrors, she would be completely fine. "It is just something I go through, *bubeleh*," she told me while stroking my cheek. "Do you think you will be able to stop? Do you think you can get help for it?" I asked Grandma Yael. Yael shook her head resolutely. "No. Such things do not leave a person's mind. The images are burned in there."

"What about going to the doctor?" I asked. Grandma Yael shook her head again. "They don't know how to treat something like what I went through. They never could," she told me.

I asked grandma Yael to tell me what happened when she was in the camp with my grandfather Elie and Papa, but she said I was too young to understand. When we finally moved, years later she would tell me some stories. She saw her two best friends – and their sons and daughters – murdered by Nazi guards in front of her eyes.

The Nazis delighted in killing children. This was only one of the stories she told me. If we would have stayed under the Soviets for longer than we did, I was sure something similar was bound to happen.

Days go by and Alek visited with some good news for Papa. He had found a tenant that was interested in renting our old apartment. By staying with grandma Yael and Grandpa Elie, we were saving our *rubles* for the big move, while also avoiding the neighbours who were spying on us. Alek arranged for the apartment to be rented by a third party. A man was hired to pretend to own the apartment. He would collect rent, and then he would give that rent to Alek who would give it to us. All of this was necessary, because if the KGB found out a Jew was making money in such a way, there was a risk the apartment could be confiscated.

I had to change schools, since I was in a completely different area of the city. To my disappointment, the school was just as cruel as the first. I did not make friends, and I was still disciplined for being Jewish. I came home on another occasion and asked grandfather Elie to teach me more about Judaism. In our new apartment, Mama decided to grow plants. She planted tomatoes and various kinds of mint. It was a fragrant corner of the apartment, and I loved sitting there and listening to Grandpa Elie.

Elie took a piece of mint and chewed on it as he spoke to me. A piece of it fell out of his mouth and got caught in his beard. "During times like these, Rebecca," he told me contemplatively. "Some Jews believe that the idea of us as a 'chosen people' should be discarded. What do you think? Do you think we should stop calling ourselves the chosen people? Do you think it is wrong to make this claim?" I thought about it. "No, I don't think it's wrong. I think the fact that they bully us in the way that they do is wrong," I said. Grandpa Elie nodded.

"That is certainly true," he said, continuing, "the belief that we are G-d's chosen people has contributed immeasurably to Jewish survival. It has enabled us to carry on in times of adversity, like we find ourselves in now. The book of Deuteronomy (7:6) clearly states that we are the chosen people. So, we must remember this and have courage."

I wondered about all the Jewish people I encountered who did not have this courage that my grandfather spoke of. My sister Lena ran away from Judaism, and Grandpa Elie knew this. There were others, people who I knew who were ashamed of being Jewish, and this disturbed me.

I asked Grandpa Elie about this, and he gave me such a cogent answer. Grandpa Elie winked at me and pated me on the head. "Let me tell you something. You can never think of an errant Jew as being lost to Judaism. There is hope, even until he is on his death bed, that a Jew who has strayed will confess his sins and repent. The door is never closed for him to come back. The law of our people states that a Jew is never denied his basic rights as a Jew, so do not worry about your sister, or your friends who are now afraid. Have hope that they will come back, and continue to be the strong young lady that I am so proud of." Grandpa Elie was so well spoken. He was so knowledgeable, and I wondered why Papa never spoke to me about his lectures.

There were hardly any Jewish students in my new school, and I missed my friend Marta. The good news was that my Mama ended up making friends with the family who lived across the hall. They too, were Jewish. It was a young family of four and the wife was strikingly beautiful. Her real name was Sephora, but she went by Daria, and she was married to an equally handsome husband, Roman.

Unfortunately, their children were too young for me to play with. They had a one-year old son and a three-year-old daughter. Their three-year-old daughter and Misha would sometimes play together. Daria and Mama would get together while I was at school, or when I arrived home.

Grandma Yael desperately wanted us all to have *Shabbat* dinner, but it was too risky. We did not know the elderly couple who lived next to us very well. Even if we did, if the elderly couple's neighbours would look down the hall and see three units congregating on a Friday night, we would raise suspicion.

One night my father came home, I could tell he was not in a good mood. He threw off his apron stained with cow blood, and sat in what was now his new chair. Grandpa Elie asked him what the matter was. "I have lost my job at the meat packing plant," he told Grandpa Elie. "Every time I think I am finally making enough *rubles*, something like this happens. I lost the job at the grocery store, and now I lost the job at the meat packing plant." Luckily, Papa always had work as a draftsman, otherwise we could not have survived as we did. But this was discouraging news.

"Tell us what happened," asked Mama. "It's aggravating," grumbled Papa. "Please, tell us," asked Mama. Papa asked to be fed first, and Mama poured him some chicken soup. This would be the last chicken soup we would eat with real chicken in it. Now we would have to go back to bones, and sometimes there were not even bones available anymore. Times were certainly getting worse.

Papa savoured the soup. It was still boiling with steam, but he slurped it down quickly. He was very hungry from working a second job, in addition to his day job as a draftsman. He knew better than any of us what losing this job meant at this time.

"I never say anything at work," he told us. I could tell he was trying to contain his rage, but it was more of a sadness than it was anger. That was the difference between agent Alexey and my Papa. He only cared for the family. He wanted to provide for us, and if he was angry, it was directed at whoever wronged him at work, not at us. I thought in this moment that I was extremely fortunate to have the parents I had. Mama and Papa were so good to me. I wondered if I had been a good daughter to them too.

Papa continued his story. "The men at work, they do not know I am Jewish, and I have purposefully kept it that way. I come into work at night. I work my shift. Then I go home. Tonight, I left my identification in my locker like I always do. Only I was so tired when I arrived at work, that I forgot to lock it."

" I left the door to my locker open, which I never do. One man, named Boris, who I believe was suspicious of me, or perhaps just wanted to steal a few *kopeks* from my wallet, went into my locker. During our five-minute break, Boris held it up and shouted at the entire lunchroom, 'look what I found. A Jew who hides amongst us. Vladimir, if that is your real name, and not your alias name. Look what his passport says, look how it says Jew on the third line.' Then everyone looked at me and the foreman called me into his office."

"They sat me down, and told me that my performance was unsatisfactory, and that the firing had nothing to do with the fact that I was Jewish. 'What Boris did was not right, but we were going to fire you anyway. We are not firing you because you are Jewish,' the foreman told me. Of course, this was a lie. My performance was exactly the same."

"Performance," Papa muttered. "There is no such thing as performance. I did the same task as a robot over and over again."

I felt terrible for Papa, and now we had to worry about money again. I anxiously wondered when we would finally escape. I wondered when Alek would come to us with good news.

Time went by, and I recall when I arrived home from school, Daria was sitting with my mother, and they were peeling potatoes together. Daria commented on how beautiful my hair was. This was not the first instance Mama's friends commented on my hair. It was naturally thick, and would make for an excellent wig. Mama had a solemn look on her face. She excused herself from Daria, and asked if she could talk with me in private.

Mama and I went into Grandma Yael's room, and sat on the mattress. Privacy was even harder to come by in our new living quarters, and it was maddening. As I grew older, I wanted my own space more and more. Mama patted the mattress, and told me to sit. She began to cry a little, but then held back her tears. "Daria has offered a decent price for your hair," she told me. "Mama, I don't want to give Daria my hair. I love my hair. She even said herself that it was beautiful." Mama gave me a big hug, and it felt good to be held by Mama like I was when I was small. It comforted me.

"I don't want you to do it either, but now we need the money. You understand, don't you Rebecca? Please tell me you understand." Mama's nose was still recovering from her awful attack at the market. The flesh around her broken nose turned from black, to blue, and now to a shiny yellow. All the sacrifice and suffering Mama endured for the family was nothing compared to me cutting off my hair. I did not need to think about the decision at all, but it still made me depressed. The one thing I loved most about my appearance was my hair.

Mama looked at me with concern and I hugged her again. "Yes, I will give Daria my hair," I said. Mama kissed me over and over again on the forehead. A tear escaped from the corner of her eye and ran down her cheek. "Soon we will leave this place. Soon we will go with Alek and we will start a new life where you will be free to have a happy family. It will not be like this forever. You will see," said Mama. "I know," I said. "I want that day to come soon, Mama. I can't wait."

Mama looked away from me as if she were ashamed. But she could not have been ashamed. She was feeling an emotion that I could not put my finger on. "I can't wait either, Rebecca," she told me.

"I have visions of our new life and I have visions of you being so happy in our new life. Remember that everything we are going though is temporary. The suffering comes and the suffering passes. Just like what happened with my nose," she said touching the bridge of her nose. "Such horrific suffering comes and then it goes. It heals, just like your hair will grow back, and the tears you cry today will turn into joy tomorrow."

Chapter Ten

The People Who Come and Go

Daria arrived the next day with a pair of gleaming scissors and a bag in which to place my hair. This was the first time I was able to see our beautiful neighbour up close. Her face was flawless. She covered her hair and face in public. She hid her face out of fear for all the harassment she would undoubtedly experience on the street from rowdy, drunken men.

I thought it was a tragedy that this had to be the case. Still, she was not as kindhearted as Mama was. She was a little bit of a hard woman. When she entered the apartment, she removed her head covering and I noticed that her hair was too beautiful to be real. Indeed, Daria wore a wig.

"Don't worry child," she said to me. "You will still be beautiful without your hair. I will give you a hat to wear. Besides, if you look like a boy for a while, it will be easier for you. The bums will not harass you as often for money to buy beer and vodka."

I did not want to watch the event. I closed my eyes and felt my braids being cut off one by one. Then she cut off my bangs. I cried and cried when it was over. "I look hideous," I told Daria. "There, there," she said. "You don't look that bad. Remember it will grow back."

I became depressed for a couple of days, looking at myself in the mirror, but ultimately, I was happy that I did it for the family. Mama and Papa thanked me and that made me feel much better for what had done. It was not long after that another financial problem plagued my parents.

The tenants in the apartment were short on the rent, and Papa could not contact the tenants directly. Alek hired a gentile middleman to collect the rent, who would give it to Alek, who would give it to my father..

Papa and Alek spoke in their usual manner at nighttime. But as always nothing they said was private. I was listening to them. Mama, Grandma Yael and Grandpa Elie probably were too. "In such a situation, there is not much that can be done," Alek told Papa. "Well," said Papa, "something must be done, because if we are not getting income, we must at least be able to pay our expenses. I just lost my second job. I don't have the money to support us, let alone pay rent for an apartment, I am not living in."

Alek agreed with this, but he had no ideas as to how to collect the rent. They agreed to sleep on it and come up with ideas later, but time was of the essence. After school, I decided to make the trip to our old apartment to see who was staying there without paying.

In hindsight, this was quite a silly decision on my part. First, as a little girl, I could do nothing to convince these people to pay. Secondly the trek to the apartment was dangerous. I could have been robbed or abducted. Luckily, I made it to the apartment safely, and I saw that the light was on.

I stood across the street looking into the window for some time. I was astonished when I finally recognized the little red-headed girl in the window. It was Marta and her family. At this point I thought I must be delusional. I thought I must be so lonely that I am imagining my friend from my past, but sure enough Marta and her family were living in our old apartment.

I knocked on the door and Marta's mother answered. Marta's mother was a plump woman, also a redhead. Her name was Yeva, and her husband's name was Yuri. They invited me in, and asked me how I was. Marta was extremely excited to see me, and I think I was just as excited to see her. We hugged and rejoiced.

A lot of our cherished items were still in the apartment. The *samovar* was still on the table and Papa's brown armchair was unmoved. We had left it during our rush to the cottage. Before anybody could speak, I asked Yeva if she saw the terrible car accident outside. "Terrible car accident? No. What happened."

"Oh, there was a terrible accident. How did you not see it? Come, I will show you," I said. I put my finger over my mouth to let them know to be silent. Then I led Yeva and her husband Yuri to the bathroom and lifted the mirror. Marta followed us. There was a piece of tape placed over the microphone. "Oh yes," whispered Yeva. "We know about the microphone. We discovered it when we moved in. We put tape over it when we have guests, but then we take it off, not to let on that we know about the bug."

Marta's family was smart. I had many questions for them, and they had many questions for me. The first question they had for me was about my hair. I took off my hat and I could see the sadness on their faces. "What happened?" asked Marta. "I had to sell it to feed the family. My Papa, he lost one of his jobs," I said. My comment seemed to give Yeva and Yuri an idea. They looked at Marta's beautiful red hair, but Marta knew exactly what they were thinking.

"Please Mama, no. I don't want to cut off my hair." Marta's mother did not say she had to, or that she did not have to, but she was certainly thinking about it. Clearly, they needed money too.

What was funny was that Marta transferred schools at the same time that I did. She was now being taught by Mrs. Berdichevsky in the school where I attended, while I was being taught in the school where Marta attended. Marta was ahead of me in school, and she offered to give me notes, which I took with me. Marta was a generous friend, indeed.

We spoke in hushed voices over dinner. Although the microphone was covered, Yeva warned us to always speak softly. I learned more about the neighbours who were paid by the KGB to spy. They had high positions with the communists, but still they needed money. Everybody needed money. It was possible they were not even antisemitic, but I highly doubted that. Eventually, I had to call my parents because they were going to wonder where I was. Marta's parents did not have a telephone, so I went to a drugstore to use the phone. The phones were also bugged by the KGB, so I had to speak carefully. "I am at Marta's place, Mama," I told my mother. "Is everything alright?" she asked. I could tell by her voice that she was worried. "Yes, everything is fine Mama. I found the *samovar* we lost. I will be home tonight."

Mama was undoubtedly confused by what I was saying, but I wanted her to know that I was safe. I returned to our old apartment and thanked them for hosting me. I could now visit my old friend as much as I wanted, and it felt wonderful to be reunited, and to have my good friend back.

As I was getting ready to leave, I realized that I had forgotten to address the issue that brought me to the apartment in the first place. The unpaid rent. I felt extremely uncomfortable bringing this issue up. I did not want to say that we still owned the apartment, or that the rent was not being paid, so I decided to keep silent and just tell Papa.

When I arrived home, my parents were terribly upset with me. "Where were you?" asked Mama. "You had us worried sick," said Papa. Grandma and Grandpa were sleeping but they awoke when they heard the commotion.

"I'm sorry, I'm sorry," I cried, "but I found out who the tenant in the apartment is. It is the family of my old friend from school, and they are Jewish. You can speak with them, Papa. You can ask about the rent, but I think they are in need of money like we are."

Papa and Mama calmed down and grandma and grandpa rubbed their eyes as they emerged from their room. "What's the matter?" yawned grandpa Elie. "Nothing, Father," said Papa. "Sorry to have woken you."

Suddenly, Grandpa Elie clutched his heart and fell to the ground. We were all shocked, and my father got down to the floor. He tried to listen to Grandpa Elie's pulse and then he tried breathing air into his mouth. I was horrified and stunned. It was as though I was frozen, and I could not move even though I wanted to. He shouted at me to call an ambulance. Luckily, grandma and grandpa's apartment had a telephone.

At the hospital, the doctor told us that Grandpa Elie had suffered a serious heart attack, and that he did not have much time to live. He was unconscious. Papa cried with Mama, and I cried too, as I held my baby brother Misha. The doctor asked Papa if he would like grandpa to be euthanized. He said they could give him a medicine to make him go to sleep forever, but Papa refused.

"If you can do surgery, do it. My father would not want to be euthanized," said Papa. Both civil law and Jewish law say that euthanasia is essentially murder. It does not matter how severe or negative the condition is. No effort should be made to shorten the life of the patient. Jewish tradition is clear that the decision of who will live or die is in G-d's hands and G-d's hands alone. Joseph Caro's Code of Jewish Law says that one is not permitted to remove a pillow from under a dying persons head, nor may one create any kind of disturbance that is likely to hasten an individual's death. Grandpa Elie taught me about Joseph Caro's Code when he gave his lectures to me.

Since this time, however, Jewish authorities have changed their mind slightly towards euthanasia. Once again, they pointed to the Talmud for clarity. When the death of Rabbi Judah the Prince, the editor of the Mishna and a prominent scholar of the third century, was imminent, his disciples gathered around his bed and prayed continuously for his recovery. One of the maid-servants who was present at the time remarked that the pain was intense, and that he was suffering. She said that it would be useless to prolong his life. She threw a jug to the ground which stunned everyone in the room, caused the praying to stop, and hastened the death of Judah.

Later, Rabbi Nissim ben Reuven Girondi who was a fourteenth-century Spanish scholar used this incident as the basis for his decision that you may refrain from praying for a sick person whose pain is intense, and for who there is no hope for recovery.

Today the Jewish authorities cite the same incident as the grounds for allowing euthanasia in certain circumstances. The argument is that when a patient is terminally ill, the doctors are not obliged to keep the patient alive using life support systems. However, they are still not allowed to use active euthanasia, which the doctor suggested for my grandfather, by injecting him with a lethal dose of sedatives.

Papa knew that the end was coming. We all knew this. I was worried about Grandma Yael. Her expression suggested that she was emotionally removed from the situation. She was the only one who was not crying, and I thought this was odd. Perhaps she could not deal with anymore death or heartache, but I knew she loved Grandpa Elie with all of her heart. Papa summoned all the strength he could muster to lift himself from the hospital chair beside my grandpa.

He told the doctor that he would like grandpa to die at home, in his own bed. The doctor agreed, and we summoned a expensive taxi service to transport us back to the apartment. The real reason Papa said this, was because he knew the hospital would not honour the Jewish customs that my grandfather would have wished for. There would be nobody allowed in the morgue to guard the body, as is the Jewish custom.

When we arrived home, Papa removed the *mezuzah* from the room where my grandfather was lying. He handed it to me, and I put it in my pocket. It was a simple *mezuzah*, and I checked inside to see the holy scroll. It was so tiny, this scroll, and I prayed to it. I prayed that Grandpa Elie would not suffer, and that the Angel of Death would be kind to him.

The Yemenites believe that the presence of holy objects lessens the power of the Angel of Death, and it makes death come sooner. Indeed, this is what happened. Within a few hours of arriving home, my dear Grandpa Elie had passed. Papa removed his shoes and started sobbing uncontrollably. Mama wrapped her arms around him, and I cried with Misha.

The Jewish funeral homes and cemeteries were constantly being desecrated during this time. The situation was so bad that there was no Jewish funeral home to take Grandpa Elie to. We did not even want to bury him in a Jewish cemetery, because vandals would come at night and kick the tombstones over.

He would have a *goyish* funeral; however, my father preformed some Jewish rituals before the coroner arrived. Papa wrapped grandpa in a cloth, and began saying the prayers for the dead. There were not enough men for a true *minyan*, which saddened my father greatly.

When the coroner came, he asked for Grandpa Elie's shoes, but my father said that we had lost them. "How could you lose someone's shoes?" asked the coroner. "I don't know. Please, just do what you need to do," said Papa.

The reality was we did not want grandpa to be cremated with shoes on. It was bad enough that he was going to be cremated, which is not at all in line with the Jewish tradition. Jews bury their dead. The communists just cremated people. The least my Papa could do was try to preserve some semblance of what Grandpa Elie would have wanted.

In the Talmud, the prophet Jeremiah left instructions to be buried in his cloths, with staff in hand, and with shoes on his feet. The reason for this was to be fully prepared for the resurrection when the Messiah would eventually come. In modern history, it is quite natural that shoes are not put on the feet of those who are to be buried. There was no proper Jewish funeral for Grandpa Elie. We received his ashes and that was that.

The entire atmosphere of our home was different now. However, years later I would be incredibly grateful for the Judaism that my grandfather instilled in me. He sparked my interest. He taught me about the important laws and customs of our people, and I am forever grateful to him for that.

Laws and customs are the mortar of Jewish life. They unify us as a people. The Torah and the Talmud are the law. The customs are the popular practice of the time. During my childhood, all our customs were repressed. This significantly impacted my generation. Jewish people like my sister Lena never recovered from such oppression. My father who was of a different generation, faced an even greater oppression than I did, but I could tell the identity was still important to him.

After the destruction of the Second Temple, ascetics proposed legislation that would prohibit the consumption of wine and meat as a sign of mourning for the loss of the Temple. Rabbi Joshua said, "No law may be established that the majority of the population cannot accept and live by." When I was old enough to read and understand Judaism further, I found such statements to be profoundly striking. Democracy and true intellectual discourse were important to the Jewish people. To the Soviets, it was not.

Although I did not understand most of what my grandfather taught me, I loved his engaging stories and explanations. I was able to ask "why" questions, and able to speak with him so freely. We were able to discuss and celebrate what it meant to be Jewish.

Soon enough there was a knock on our door. It was our next-door neighbour, the elderly neighbour who we did not know. Mama wiped her tears away and tried to compose herself before opening the door. We were all still devastated over what happened to my grandfather. In the hallway was a short elderly woman with gold stud earrings, and curly white hair. She had an unusual accent, and presented Mama with a bunch of grapes, a rare treat we hadn't seen since last summer at the cottage.

Grapes were a delicacy. The kind lady offered her sympathies, and asked us if we were sitting *shiva*. "Are you Jewish?" Mama asked her. "Yes," said the woman. We were relieved that she was

Jewish. This meant we did not have to hide as much as we did before. We invited her inside and she introduced herself as Berta. Berta had a husband that was quite ill, and she had a strange accent. Berta was a new neighbour, as the neighbours before her were not Jewish, and they spied on Grandpa Elie and Grandma Yael though the wall, which caused them to observe *Shabbat* dinner at my parent's old apartment.

Berta was one of the kindest ladies I met when I was a child. She also liked children, and she had a family, although they were in America, and she longed to see them one day. After she spoke with Mama and Papa, she retired to her apartment, and Daria came over to give her condolences to Grandma Yael, Mama, and Papa.

After the death of Grandpa Elie, Grandma Yael was not the same. She became withdrawn, and her night terrors only got worse. This was understandable. We had only been mourning the loss of my grandfather for a few days when Papa realized that we did not have enough money to cover the bills until the end of the month.

He needed to speak to Marta's family about the rent. I felt so bad for my Papa during this time. He had to work, mourn his father, and deal with the bills. On top of all this, he also had secret work to perform for Alek. Mama knew more than I did, but even Mama did not know the details of what Papa was working on.

All Papa told us was that he was working hard with Alek to secure "all of the necessary paperwork." I imagined this included bribing more communist party members and securing more money from our friends in the United States and Canada.

Papa returned to the apartment during this time, and he was completely exhausted. The dark bags under his eyes were heavier than I had ever seen them. He sat down in his chair and Mama fed him while I took care of Misha. I was feeding Misha some of the leftovers from dinner that I had cut up for him into tiny cubes. Papa told Mama that he had good news and bad news.

"Well, start with the good news," said Mama. Papa inhaled and then exhaled slowly. "The good news is that Marta's family had been paying the rent. In fact, they have been paying slightly more per month than what we were charging." Mama became confused when she heard this, and I did too. We were not receiving the rent. We were short, hence our unfortunate financial situation.

Papa nodded, "Yes I know, I was puzzled when they told me this as well. Then I quickly realized what was happening. The man who Alek had hired to pose as the non-Jewish landlord was stealing a substantial portion of the rent for himself. His name is Markiyan. Every month he collects rent from Marta's family, as well as many other families, and many times he hands over the money to people like Alek for a small fee. We are not the only Jews who own property."

"Makiyan found quite the niche market, and made a profitable business for himself. Only now he is getting greedy, and my estimate is that he doesn't care if we know that he is stealing."

"How do you know that?" asked Mama. Papa shrugged. "I don't know that for sure, but I'm going to speak with him." Mama crossed her arms. She did not like that idea at all, and neither did I. "We must think first before we speak with him. What if he reports us to the KGB? They could confiscate our property. He has a lot of power. We need to be smart."

Papa listened to what Mama was saying. My grandmother was listening to the conversation too, but she was now in her own world. I had no doubt that she was still reeling from the death of my grandfather. After all, we all were. Papa too. It was good that Mama was able to listen to Papa and tell him to think first, considering his state of mind. G-d knows what could have happened if he just approached Markiyan with no plan. Papa decided to contact the only person he could in a situation such as this, his good friend Alek.

Mama made tea and I managed to get those lovely sugar cubes I had tasted once before. I can't remember how I managed to acquire such a treat, but I did, and my parents appreciated it. Grandma Yael just sucked on the cubes out of the package without tea. I was beginning to become worried about her.

Alek and Papa discussed what the best course of action was regarding Markiyan. Alek snapped his fingers. "Ah ha! It's so simple, Vladimir," he said to my father with a smile of contentment on his face. "Simply tell Marta's family to stop paying Markiyan. Markiyan will stop paying me, and you will collect the rent directly from Marta's family. We will just cut him out. I will fire him."

Papa became nervous when he heard this. "Yes," he said. "But what if Markiyan finds out? He will report all of us." Alek laughed. "Markiyan will not find out. How could he? I will tell him his services are no longer needed to collect rent, and that will be that. He can still collect rent for other Jewish landlords, just not yours."

The plan seemed to be good, and shortly afterwards Alek fired Markiyan, but our troubles were only beginning. As Papa feared, he did not simply go away. The rent he was collecting from Marta's family made a difference to him. Papa made a trip the next week to collect the rent, and on his way home, he was followed by Markiyan, only he did not know he was being followed.

Papa arrived home and dumped the *rubles* and *kopeks* on my grandmother's bed. "See! Now our troubles are over. Now we will have enough to purchase the last certificates we need to get out of this place and finally leave the Soviet Union." I had never seen

Papa so happy. Almost immediately after Papa had said this and we all rejoiced at the thought of freedom from the Soviets, there was a loud knock on our apartment door.

It was Markiyan, a short tubby man with a large belly and the most hideous ears I had ever seen. His ears were far too large for his face, and he had greedy little black slits for eyes. "Ah ha! So, you are the owner of 1556, unit 1B. I found you," he said to Papa, grinning. "You think you could just cut me out? Well it is not that simple. I know who you are now." He peered underneath my Papa's arm which was blocking the doorway to the apartment, and he grinned again when he saw me and Misha. "I know your family now too. Now, do not be afraid. I am a reasonable man. We are both businessmen you and I, so I have an arrangement I would like to propose. You give me eighty percent of the rent, and I will not report you to the KGB for practicing your vile religion like the rats that you are."

Papa grabbed Markiyan by the throat and began to suffocate him. Mama shouted at Papa to let him go, but he would not. He had threatened our family, and Papa mustered all his strength and squeezed Markiyan even harder. I was terrified, of course, and I was frozen, just as I had been frozen when Grandpa Elie died.

Papa walked with Markiyan with his hands on his throat towards the stairwell at the end of the hallway where our unit was. He pressed Markiyan against the door, then released his grip on his throat. "You are not going to threaten my family," Papa shouted at Markiyan. Markiyan gasped and laughed. He spat in Papa's face. "You dirty Jew. You don't get to tell me what to do. Just because you put your filthy Jewish rat hands on me, I'm going to report all of you to the KGB and take all of the rent for myself. Then you will see what will happen to your children! You will all be exiled to Siberia or somewhere worse!"

Papa was angry and pushed Markiyan. He fell backwards down the stairs. He hit his head multiple times and fell onto the landing in the stairwell of the apartment building. We all rushed over to see if he was okay, but he was unconscious.

At this point the entire hallway was alerted to the altercation. Berta and Daria came out first, as they were the closest neighbours. Mama blocked the doorway to the stairwell and told Daria to block the entrance, so that the other neighbours would not see what happened. Daria and Berta did exactly that, and the ambulance was called.

Markiyan was seriously injured, and taken to the hospital. He was unconscious but the doctors said that he should wake up soon. Papa was sick with worry at home. He did not leave the house. "If they found out he died because of me, a Jew, that's it for us. We will all be exiled to Siberia. Our family is done," I heard Papa say to my mother in grandmother's bedroom. I was with my grandmother Yael and Misha, listening to them speak.

"If he wakes up, that might even be worse for us," said Papa. Mama was clearly worried, but tried to comfort Papa. "We don't know anything yet. Let us wait and see what happens."

The pressure was now on for us to leave the country. There was the threat of Markiyan and the time imperative of the necessary paperwork. The Soviet Jews only had a small window in which to leave. We had to move quickly.

Chapter Eleven

The Tickets

We anxiously waited to see if Markiyan would recover, or stay unconscious in the hospital. We desperately hoped he would not report us. We also desperately hoped he would not die. Papa could not handle the guilt of killing a man. He was far too sensitive for that.

Meanwhile, Alek continued to make significant progress regarding securing the proper paperwork. Alek and my father met more regularly than ever. Papa needed to give him money to bribe the communist officials for the remainder of the documents.

Luckily, we now had the money from the rent from Marta's parents, and the little money we had from my parents' salary. Grandma Yael whispered to me when Papa and Mama were not looking. She told me to sit on the mattress and be still. Then she reached underneath the mattress and produced a tin of shoe polish.

"What is it?" I asked her. "My child, look inside, but hide your excitement. Don't let your parents hear you, okay?" I was excited.

I opened the tin to find a stash of coins. *Kopeks* and *rubles* tucked neatly into a folded piece of cloth. "I have been saving little by little over the years. Nobody knows about it, but it will be good to keep on our journey. I want you to keep it in case I die," she told me. I thought this was a horrible thing to say, but Grandma Yael was a realist. She knew what it was like to go through the camps, and she hoarded items for survival.

Eventually Alek did have news regarding Markiyan, although I was not at home at the time to hear it. I was at school. When I returned home, I learned the news from Mama. She had prepared a celebratory desert for us to eat. A platter of fruits and tea. She told me that Markiyan had woken up in the hospital, and was terrified to see our friend, Alek, standing over his hospital bed. Before Alek could say anything to Markiyan, he promised not to say anything to the KGB and to refrain from harming Papa or taking any of his money. Papa scared him off, and that was the end of it. When Papa heard this news, he was overjoyed. All of us were overjoyed. We thought we would certainly be reported or worse, but it worked out for the best. We were incredibly lucky.

One evening Alek pulled up outside Grandma Yael's apartment in his red car, and did not look pleased. Instead of talking in secrets, he addressed all of us. "There are some issues with the visas I have obtained," said Alek. His forehead was wrinkled with lines of worry. "We have the right to leave the country, but the right to go to Israel is a different story. Many members of the Jewish community have been granted access to leave for Israel, but now, there simply are not enough visas for all of us."

Papa looked concerned and so did Mama. "So, what does that mean?" Mama finally asked. Alek sighed. "It means if we want to leave as soon as possible, we have to leave for Italy, and then go to America. But if we want to go to Israel, we have to stay for another six months at least."

Clearly, there was no decision to make. We had to leave for Italy immediately. Mama knew this, and even at my young age, I knew this too. We were astonished when Papa hesitated. "Perhaps we should wait to go to Israel. Perhaps it is worth the wait," he said slowly.

"That's crazy!" shouted Mama. Misha started crying and I consoled him and fed him some beans from the pantry. "Why crazy?" asked Papa. Mama could hardly contain herself. Grandma Yael just watched us from her bed. Mama used her hands to talk. She was so upset with Papa. "We can't risk it. That is why it is crazy to stay. Every day we wait in this place, we are in more and more danger. We need to get out as soon as possible."

Papa had no choice to agree. It was the most rational thing to do. The hatred towards Jews was increasing by the day. Mama was right. Alek nodded resolutely. "Very well, I shall prepare everything by the end of the week, Vladimir," he told Papa. "Prepare to leave in two weeks."

There was a lot we needed to do in the two weeks we had left under the Soviets. We needed to pack, and decide what to leave behind. We knew that we could not sell the apartment or the cottage. The communists would confiscate them, but this was a small price to pay for our freedom.

I sat in class and felt absolutely giddy that I would soon leave this place, this school, and this life for a new one. The teachers are all a blur to me now, and so are the students. I just remember sitting in my classroom in the first weeks of March and seeing a spectacular spring day outside.

Immediately after school ended, I walked to our old apartment where Marta and her family now lived. They were relieved to be paying Papa rent instead of that horrible man who stole from us. In fact, we were able to charge slightly less rent, because we were receiving the money directly from Marta's family.

They invited me to sit in Papa's old chair, and I told Marta, her mother, and her father that our family was leaving to Italy. Marta was terribly upset with me, which shocked me. "How could you leave? You are my only friend. Why wouldn't your parents wait until they can go to Israel?" Marta asked me in tears. I did not know how to respond. I did not want to say, because it was dangerous to continue to live under the Soviets. If I were to say that, it would be rude. Luckily, Marta's mother answered for me. "Darling, we will all get out soon enough. You should be happy for your friend. Tell her congratulations!"

Marta's eyes were a different shade of bloodshot red than her hair. She hugged me very tightly and I wanted to cry too. She was my best friend. The worst part of it was that I could not contact her when we would arrive in Italy. It was extremely dangerous to send communications this way, because the KGB would intercept everything.

If I told Marta in my letter about the wonderful new life, they would confiscate the communication, or punish Marta and her family. Our parents knew better than we did that if we said goodbye, that would likely bet the end of it. I would never see her again. It would be as though nothing existed. Not our hardships. Not our friendships. Everything would be erased as though it never happened. This was a most terrifying feeling to experience. The feeling of non-existence.

It seemed as though there was nothing else to say to my friend Marta, except that it was lovely to have known her, and that I was grateful for the friendship we had. Except, there was the unresolved issue of the apartment.

Her mother tapped me on my back as I said a tearful goodbye. "Ask your father about the apartment. If you are leaving, we need to know where that leaves us. We need to know if we can still stay here, after the Soviets take it." I was not thinking about such things at this time. I was emotional, and Marta's mother brought up a very good point. I would have to do this one last errand for my friend.

When I arrived home my parents, were in a frenzy. They were making a list of everything we needed for the journey. It was decided that we would take a train to Italy, and we were waiting for Alek to arrive with the tickets and our papers. I asked Papa about Marta and her family.

"What do we tell Marta? Where will her family go, Papa?" Papa looked concerned. He had not thought of that. There was so much on his mind during this time. Mama and Papa were ready to give up the apartment and the cottage, but neither one of them thought about Marta.

Papa knelt down to speak to me. He never did this. I think he was impressed that I thought of such a thing during such a stressful time. "Go back and tell them that they can move in here, when the Soviets confiscate the apartment. Grandma Yael has already paid for next month's rent. So, they can have a month of free rent, and then keep paying as though they had always lived here." It was a brilliant idea.

I ran back to Marta's place to tell them the good news, and her parents were ecstatic. Marta's mother produced the *samovar* that Mama cherished, and that we had lost when we moved to the cottage. "This was in the apartment when we moved in. You should take it back to your Mama and Papa," she told me. "Please tell them that we are so thankful for their generosity."

I told them that I would, and I hid the *samovar* in multiple cloths Marta's mother gave me. It was not safe to carry such a valuable item through the streets and for such a long distance. When I arrived home, I was quite exhausted, but there was no time to rest. I had to plan for a party for the next day. I hid the *samovar* beneath the mattress along with Grandma Yael's tin of money.

We would have a party with our neighbours Berta and Daria the next day. It was our last day in Grandma Yael's apartment. Our last day before we set out on our quest to be free. Mama and Daria prepared a wonderful meal, and Berta brought many special fruits that she saved for an occasion such as this. We had the party in the middle of the day, which was unusual. I was not in school, and Papa was not working. Everyone was home and it was lovely.

There was only one person missing, my beloved sister Lena. I wondered where she was. I did not know if she was going to come to the party. I did not even know if she was going to come with us. Nobody told me anything, and it was infuriating. They knew I was a curious child, and so they kept as much information from me as possible now. They knew I had a mind of my own. They knew what I would do if I found out Lena was never planning on escaping with us.

Even though my sister and I did not have the best relationship due to the age gap, I still loved her deeply. It was devastating that she did not come with us. This is what made the party so bittersweet in my memory. Lena rang the doorbell before Daria and Berta showed up. She hugged Mama, Papa, Grandma Yael, Misha and me. She told us that she wished us the best in our new life and that she loved us very much.

"You never tell us anything about your life," I complained. "You come and go for months without so much as a letter or a visit.

Why won't you come with us? Why won't you come?" I pleaded with my sister. Lena could not look me in the eye. She was still defeated. She was still ashamed of being Jewish, and she was still involved with her mysterious husband who we hardly ever saw. She was also still quite young. Barely into her early twenties. There was so much potential for her, but she did not have enough strength to leave her husband and come with us.

Lena clasped my hands in hers. "There is a lot you do not understand, Rebecca," she told me. "So, tell me! What is it I don't understand?" Lena kissed me on the forehead. "I have a life here. I have a husband, and it is not as difficult for you as it is for me. Papa and Mama will take care of you until you are old enough to find a husband. You will be all right, and I will be all right."

This answer did not satisfy me at all. It certainly did not satisfy my parents, but there was nothing we can do except to beg her and plead with her to come with us.

Although she was in her twenties, in retrospect, she was also just a child. I wish Papa would have dragged her with us. For many years I wondered about Lena, and I cried for her too.

My sister left us, and told us she would come to the train station the next day to say our final goodbyes. Daria and Berta came over shortly after Lena had left, and we began the party, but everyone was understandably somber. "What's the matter?" Daria asked Mama. Daria had a profound emotional intelligence. I could tell that she knew how to read people as she cut my hair those many weeks before. "Oh, we are all just a little upset that Lena has decided to stay," said Mama melancholically.

Daria hugged Mama and told her that it was all right. Sometimes, in such a circumstance, there was not much that could be said. Papa did not say anything, but this is how he dealt with incomprehensible grief. He buried it away, like the memories of the concentration camps.

He would never speak about such distressing events. In this time people rarely spoke openly about their feelings. I was different. I was a rebel.

Mama asked Daria to get the door when Berta knocked. Then Daria said something refreshing to Mama. "Call me by my Hebrew name. Call me Sephora," she said, with a contented smile that sticks in my mind to this day. A wonderfully contented smile, like the one on the Mona Lisa. This was after all, a celebration. We were finally going to be able to be who we really were. Jews.

Berta came and brought wonderful grapes and slices of cheese for us to eat. This was a wonderful treat. Then I decided it was time to reveal what I had recovered from Marta's apartment. I whispered to Mama and Papa to follow me, but of course everyone heard, and watched me as I dug under Grandma Yael's mattress to produce the *samovar*.

Mama jumped up and nearly hit the ceiling. "How did you get it back?" she exclaimed. "Marta's family found it when they moved in. They saved it for us Mama, isn't it wonderful?"

Mama prepared the *samovar* and we all sat around the table, wondering what life would be like in Italy. We were still waiting for Alek to come to us with the tickets and documents. Sephora revealed that she was going to Israel in two weeks from the day we departed. In a way, we were also celebrating Sephora's departure as well.

Berta was too old to leave. Her husband was sick, and she was too weak to make the journey, but she was happy for us. Berta was a selfless and caring person. We were extremely fortunate to have found such good friends, and it would be very difficult, especially for Mama, to leave them behind.

There was a particular kinship formed with people who shared the same language and Jewish identity, especially during the time we spent under the Soviets. The fact that it was dangerous to show one's true identity, strengthened the bonds we formed with people like Sephora and Berta. We all drank tea, and Grandma Yael began to play with her tealeaves once she had consumed all of the liquid.

"I will read your fortune," she told me playfully. She looked at my tea leaves and then examined the lines of my hand, "Oh yes. Yes," said Grandma Yael. "You have long lifelines in your palm, and the tea leaves say you will live a very long life, and marry a wonderful husband. You will also become very rich," she said playfully. "That's silly, you can't tell all of that from tea leaves," I told Grandma Yael. "Ah, she's a smart girl," said Grandma Yael, winking at me.

My grandmother picked up on the joyous mood of the party. She smiled for the first time in a long time, since before Grandpa Elie died. I helped Mama clean and took care of Misha after the party was over. Sephora and Berta promised to see us off the next day, and we continued to wait for Alek to arrive.

We nervously waited for a couple of hours and Papa was visibly anxious. "Where is he?" he muttered to himself. "I hope nothing is wrong," said Mama. The mood was such a contrast to just hours before.

After all these months of planning and suffering, the only thing that separated us from freedom was the ticket out. Perhaps it was naiveté, but I never doubted Alek. He always followed through. I knew he would come, and sure enough, he did.

In the late afternoon, I heard Alek's red car pull up in front of our building. I looked out the window to see him hurrying towards the apartment with an envelope tucked tightly underneath his brown spring jacket.

"I have the tickets and I have the exit visas. The only thing I need is all of your passports," he told Papa. "We need to surrender all of our passports to the communists when boarding the train. The destination is Rome, Italy, but the train will first travel through Chop, Zakarpattia Oblast, near the border of Hungary. The journey will be long, but worthwhile," said Alek. Papa grabbed our passports and put them all on the table for Alek to collect. He placed them in another envelope, and handed Papa our tickets.

This was it. We were finally going to leave for a better life. At this time, we did not know what would come after Italy. We thought we might go to Israel or the United States, but we had no idea. All that was on Mama and Papa's mind, but at this time, it was leaving the communists behind.

"It is not safe for me to return to my apartment," Alek told my father. "Can I sleep here tonight?" Papa scoffed. "What kind of question is that? Of course, you can. Take Rebecca's bed and she can sleep with us or on the floor." I was happy to give my bed to Alek. He was our saviour, our hero.

Our train was scheduled to depart early in the morning. Mama and Papa told me and Grandma Yael to go to bed early, although we could not sleep. The only one who could sleep was Misha. He did not understand what was happening around us, and perhaps it was for the best. Our journey was about to begin, and it was not going to be as simple or as easy as I thought.

My bag was exceptionally light. I had one change of clothing, and my school uniform, which I had learned to despise. Still, one change of clothing was not enough, so I carried the uniform with me just in case my other clothing became stained. The bottoms were a plain grey and the top had our flag sown into the breast pocket. If I needed another pair of bottoms, I would simply use my school uniform and discard the top.

I slept with Grandma Yael, and she tossed and turned all through the night, not allowing me to sleep. She screamed a few times. "Get your hands off me," she screamed. "No, no no!"

She was still dreaming of the Nazi guards. I prayed that I would not have to sit or sleep next to Grandma Yael on the train, otherwise I would not get very much sleep. When the morning came, Papa was the first to rise.

All the suitcases were by the door. We only had a few valuable items that we carried with us. The *samovar,* a vase Mama liked that had painted flowers on it, some silver coins, and some drafting supplies that Papa thought was valuable. I also took two blue books of Grandpa Elie's with me in my suitcase to read. Papa kept a hidden wallet in a secret contraption under his pants, where he kept all our money. I also kept the tin grandma Yael gave me in my underwear, since I did not have the same contraption that Papa did.

I think Papa struggled to leave his beloved radio behind. Before we left the apartment for good, he touched the radio and said a little prayer. I rarely saw Papa pray. Perhaps he was praying for our safety.

Everything fit into Alek's tiny red car, which was astonishing to me. He had to slam the trunk closed, but it fit. Berta came downstairs to say goodbye to us on the street before we left. "I wish I had the strength to see you off at the station," she told us. "But I wish you all the luck in the world. You have a beautiful family," she told Mama. "Enjoy the new life in the new country. Make the most of it." Mama and Berta hugged, and Misha sat on my lap.

Sephora ran downstairs, her hair was uncombed, and she looked like she had just woken up. "I nearly missed you! Take care darling. May G-d bless you and watch over you and the family," she told Mama. She also recited the prayer for safe travel, which calmed Mama more than it calmed Papa. They hugged and kissed. This would be the last time we ever saw Sephora or Berta. This was the most difficult part about leaving for Mama. Leaving her friends and family behind.

Alek tried to start the car, but it would not start. "Not now!" he shouted. He hit the dashboard out of frustration. The cars were unreliable back then, and the gauges were unreliable too. One almost had to possess the skills of a mechanic to own and operate a simple passenger car.

Luckily, Papa was skilled with his hands. The two of them looked under the hood and quickly identified the problem with the motor. I could not repeat what was wrong with it, as I had no idea what they were talking about. Papa rifled through his suitcase and produced one of his drafting tools which I recognized. It was a square shaped tool used for drawings, and he shoved it inside a component of the motor.

Alek tried to start the motor again and miraculously, it worked. The little red car roared to life and carried us almost all the way to the station before the motor started sputtering and producing a thick grey smoke. Then a horrible buzzing sound came on, and the engine died about two blocks away from the station. We left the car there, on the side of the road. There was no time to notify anyone or call for a repair.

Alek swore, and we had to walk the rest of the way. I carried Misha, and Mama carried two suitcases. We were afraid we were going to miss our train, but we made it in time. To my delight, I saw Marta standing on the platform, looking around frantically.

"Marta!" I exclaimed. Marta ran and hugged me. She told me that her parents wanted to come, but they had to work. "What about school? Won't you be late for school?" I asked Marta. "I don't care, they will punish me one way or another," she told me.

I held my friend Marta and I told her that I wished she could come with us. Marta told me she also wished she could go. "Maybe we will meet again in Israel," she told me. I began to cry. I could not stand to lose another friend, but I had learned that this was the way things were. Friends came and friends went.

"I really hope so," I said through my tears. "I really hope I do see you in Israel. You are my best friend, Marta," I told her. I had never told anyone that before. Not Alex, not Alla, not anyone. Marta was truly my best friend. "You are *my* best friend," said Marta. "Please promise me you will write me when you get to Italy." I did not know what to say. I could not promise such a thing because I did not know. "I will try," I said. Just saying I would try rather than promising that I would, made me feel horrible. I felt as though I should have promised, but it was good that I did not promise.

Later Mama would catch me writing a letter to Marta on the train, but she would throw it away in the trash, saying, "this letter could be dangerous to Marta and her family if you send it. You must wait until it is safe to communicate with her." There would never be a time when it was "safe." I never heard from Marta again after that day at the train station. This was the way things were at that time. It tore my heart out at the time.

We kept our tickets with us, because there were officials on the train whose job it was to inspect everyone's ticket. Alek surrendered all our passports, and Papa displayed the visas to a communist party official, who guarded the entrance to the train.

He wore a hat very similar to that of Alexey, and he inspected the exit visas that Papa gave him. Papa's foot was trembling as I stood behind him and Alek. Mama was beside me, and I was holding little Misha's hand as he squirmed. Grandma Yael was fanning herself because it was hot outside for March. The sun was shining down on us that day, and she looked weak. Her skin was a strange tinge of yellow, which worried me.

The communist party official nodded at Papa. "All right, you can climb aboard. Go ahead." We boarded the train with all of our belongings. The space inside the train was cramped and the air was stifling. We were fortunate enough to be given seats by the window. Papa and Alek lifted all our belongings up, and onto a narrow shelf where we all sat. The shelf was open, so everyone could see what we were carrying. This made Mama, Papa, and Alek very nervous. Grandma Yael did not look well, so she sat across from Misha and I, to get the air from the window.

We were amongst the first families on the train. Shortly after we boarded, more and more families came on, and the passenger train was absolutely packed full of people. Most of the passengers were families like us, but there were also single people and strange characters who looked suspicious.

After ten to fifteen minutes, the train blew its horn for the final time, and the car jerked forward. I was extremely excited to be moving. Grandma Yael looked nauseous. She was not used to riding in a train. Mama, Papa, and Alek spoke about this and that, but I was focused on what was happening outside. I would focus on our fellow travelers later.

Chapter Twelve

The Train to Italy

For the first few hours of our train ride, I was mesmerized by the countryside. The train chugged along, winding, and twisting in-between large, white mountain ranges, and a spectacular blue sky.

There were wildflowers which grew next to the train tracks, and I would count how many different shades of lilac there were. Streams of water spilled from the top of the mountains and fell into the bed of shallow rivers. I would track the zig zag pattern of the streams that fell off the mountains, and watch how they would disrupt the beautiful farmland. We must have passed hundreds of farms on our way to Italy.

Even after hours of looking out the window, we had still not crossed the border into Hungary. I wondered what Budapest would look like. Misha continued to squirm and cry. It was not easy for a small child to sit in one place for that long, but it was very difficult to walk with him due to the limited space in the train. I had to hold him down and calm him.

The same agent who inspected our exit visas slammed the door to our car, and shouted at everyone to hold their tickets up so that he could see. Papa held all our tickets up, and Alek held his ticket up as well. He passed with no problem. There was also militia on board the train, which made Papa nervous.

"I will feel better when we are finally in Italy," whispered Papa to Mama. Mama nodded in agreement. Alek did not say much; he was weary, and he tilted the brim of his hat down over his tired blue eyes to sleep. Alek had lost weight in the past number of weeks. My father too. To arrange everything was quite stressful, and finding a new place to live in Italy would also be stressful. Although the train ride was not comfortable or relaxing in the slightest for my parents, or for Alek, at least they did not have to worry about food, money, or a place to stay, for now. All those worries would come later.

Eventually, my attention did shift to the characters who we were riding with. Many of them were families like us, but many were not.

Sitting across the aisle from us was a single man who kept looking at our *samovar* and all our valuables. Mama noticed him first and alerted Papa by nudging him. "He keeps looking at our things," whispered Mama. Papa took a careful glance at the man across from us and yawned.

"He looks like he might be with the militia, or perhaps a spy with the KGB. Just don't pay attention to him," Papa whispered back. "Try to sleep," added Papa. Papa and Alek fell asleep quite quickly, but Mama could not sleep. Mama and I both looked over at the mysterious man every once in a while.

He did not break his stare. His presence was unnerving us. Eventually he rose from his seat and walked across the nearly nonexistent isle. The space between isles was exceedingly small.

Mama nudged Papa to wake up. This time she nudged him quite forcefully out of fear. Papa was startled by the man who spoke in a low and throaty Hungarian accent.

"Excuse me miss," he addressed Mama. "I could not help but notice your wonderful vase with the beautifully painted flowers. I would like to buy it from you," he said.

The man looked intimidating when he was staring at us from across the aisle, but now he seemed friendly. He introduced himself as "Robert" and he was traveling to Budapest where his family lived. He was dignitary for the government, and this impressed Mama and Papa. Astonishingly, Alek slept through Robert's introduction.

I knew Mama did not want to sell her vase. It was the one of the few beautiful objects she owned, but we needed as much money we could get. I could also tell she did not want to be rude to this man. He instructed us that he was a dignitary, but he could very well have been a spy for the KGB.

Mama asked what Robert would offer for it. "I can pay you a fair price," said Robert. In his hand were a few paper bills. Mama's eyes widened when she saw the payment. "Is that enough?" Robert asked Mama. "Oh yes," said Mama. "More than enough."

Robert clapped his hands and laughed. "Very good. I now have a present for my wife when I return home. She will be a happy little lady. Perhaps she will even make me beef stroganoff. That is my favourite meal," said Robert.

We did not know what Robert was talking about, but we were happy to have the money he offered us. Grandma Yael looked to be dehydrated and Papa told me to fetch her some water. Instead, Robert offered the water that he had with him. "I wish her good health," said Robert.

I thought that I would recognize more families on the train than I did. One of the families who were seated further down the car was from my first school. Their son was in Mrs. Berdichevsky's class with me. I was not friends with the boy, but I did know he was Jewish like we were. There were lots of Jews on the train. Some of them went to Italy and stayed there. Others went to Israel. It was good that we were getting out. The antisemitism of the Soviets would only worsen as the years went on. I was happy that we got out just in time.

It took quite a while to get to Budapest. Time passed slowly, because there was not a lot to do on the train except to read and sleep. The other passengers ate sunflower seeds, and they threw them on the floor when they were done. This made the floor of the train absolutely disgusting. People also smoked cigarette after cigarette. I was not used to this. Mama and Papa did not smoke. The other passengers also smelled. They did not shower for days, so the stench of the car was horrendous.

The only reprieve we got was when the train would stop in a small town, and the doors would swing open. Some passing townsfolk would look at us with curiosity, and even revulsion. I could not blame them. I would have the same reaction to these strange people from the city.

When I got tired from looking out the window, or I was not busy tending to Misha, or speaking with Mama, or Papa, or Grandma Yael, I would read Grandpa Elie's books. I wondered if we would have the opportunity to celebrate the high holidays in our new country.

We could barely observe the *Shabbat* in the proper manner under the Soviets. I was so curious about the high holidays, and all I knew about them were from the stories Grandpa Elie told me. It was almost April, and the closest holiday was Passover. We never observed Passover, so I went through Grandpa Elie's book and decided to read about it. Passover began as, and remains, a family holiday.

The array of delicacies associated with family Seder celebrations, as well as the foods prepared for the rest of Passover, continue to attract family members to share in the experience.

I began reading about it in the book.

Exodus 12 says, God said to Moses and Aaron: "this month, the month of Nissan, shall be unto you the beginning of months. On the tenth day of this month they, the children of Israel, shall take to every man a lamb, according to their father's household." It was fascinating to read Grandpa Elie's book, and reading his book reminded me of his warmth and good humor. I missed him greatly, and I missed sitting with him and learning from him and asking him questions.

I did not attend my first Passover Seder until we would arrive in Italy, and it would not even be with my own family. It would be with a friend. Still, I enjoyed reading about the holiday. Just like Shavuot and Sukkot, this holiday is a major one. It is a distinctive and meaningful holiday. A holiday that symbolizes in words and deeds the ideal of freedom. I thought this was so fitting that I read about this wonderful holiday as my family and I were becoming free, just like the slaves of Egypt.

The train pulled into the station in Budapest, and Robert wished us a good journey, as he took Mama's floral vase. It had been a long journey and Papa said we should all exit the train to get some fresh air. We gazed upon what must have been the Danube River, Europe's second-longest river, after the Volga. It flows through ten countries, and it was a magnificent site to behold. We were thankful that we got to breathe fresh air. Grandma Yael was particularly relieved.

Though the city was beautiful, we did not have time to take in the sights. It was just a stop over, and the train continued, crisscrossing between the border of Austria and Slovenia. The spring flowers in a wet year were fragrant and more beautiful than any other flowers I had ever seen.

I gazed out the window of the train and noticed that the coloured flowers seemed brighter if there were a few white flowers to give the colours definition. Every petal of those marvelously blue flowers was edged with white, so that a field of them is bluer than you can imagine. The land was rich and deep, and seemed to go on into infinity.

The men and women who looked like spies, militia or KGB slowly left the train, stop by stop; as we progressed on our journey, they left the train. Soon, most of the car contained passengers like us.

Jews, looking for a better life. When we left Budapest, there were more Hungarians on the train. When we arrived in Austria, there were more Austrians. We watched the passengers come and go, and I wondered what all their stories were.

Mama, Papa, and Alek all made a point not to speak with anyone if they did not have to. It still wasn't safe for us. We had to be careful. Alek still had the silver-plated lighter in the breast pocket of his blue button-down shirt. He had worn the same shirt many times, since I first met him during our New Year's party, in what seemed like ages ago.

He flicked the top of the lighter open and closed, trying to synchronize the clicking and clacking of the top of the lighter to the sound of the train tracks. Alek smiled at me from his seat. "So, little Rebecca. Tell me, what do you want to be when you grow up?" I was surprised to hear Alek's voice. He had been silent for most of the journey. At this age, everything was simpler.

Everything was so much clearer to me. I answered immediately. "I want to be a mother," I told him. Alek grinned at me in a friendly way. The sun shined through the glass of the train car and illuminated his deep blue eyes. "Really? You want to be a mother? Not a secret agent?"

I laughed. I had always known him to be very serious, but now he was making jokes. Perhaps it was because we were almost in Italy. The excitement was building, and I could no longer concentrate on reading. I grew impatient with taking care of Misha. I just wanted to arrive already.

When we finally crossed the border into Italy, there was no way to tell. It was not until the train reached the coast that we noticed the Italian signs, and Italian language spoken on board the train.

The train rounded a mountain bend and we could see the magnificent Tyrrhenian Sea. As we looked out the window, we saw a long, turquoise beach glimmered in the foreground, stretching spectacularly in front of our almost disbelieving, delighted eyes. The edge of the sea ran parallel with the rails, and so near that the breezes blew flecks of foam from the waves into our faces.

Misha and I laughed with delight. "Mama, I smell the sea!" I shouted excitedly. "Look how beautiful everything is!" Mama looked uncertain. She looked over at Papa. "I want to swim there," Misha declared. Misha wanted to jump off the train and, fully clothed, and jump into the sea.

We were perhaps only near Pisa or Florence. The train still had to make the journey down to coast to Rome, but Alek assured us that it was not much longer until we got there. I kept staring at the sea. It was wonderful. The sunlight was wonderful too. Grandma Yael put her face in the sun pouring in from the window, and smiled. I gave her a big hug. We all felt a little better.

Just like Alek said, within a brief time, we arrived in Rome. The whistle blew and the conductor tried to get people off the train as we stepped down. I gazed around me at the wealthy private villas, huge apartment buildings, and enormous private properties right on the beach.

Chapter Thirteen

Rome

When we arrived in Rome, we were struck by how happy and fashionable the people were. In the 1970s, Rome was the embodiment of *la dolce vita* (the sweet life). Their economy was doing exceptionally well, and even the movie industry from America was filming there. A famous film which I would see years later was filmed in Italy, *Ben Hur*. It was a spectacular film for the time.

I visited the iconic Cincecitta Studios and watched in awe as a few movie stars strolled in and out. We walked the sunny streets of Rome for some time. "Some people just do not realize how lucky they are!" Papa lamented.

Rome's street traffic was awful and loud, but lively. The pedestrian traffic was full of people walking arm-in-arm and looking incredibly happy.

"It's probably not bad here at all," Papa said, looking around.

Every few minutes I saw a black Mercedes pass and blow its horn at the people walking by. We saw people walking on the roads, eating at side cafes – everyone was enjoying the hot weather. We were astounded by all the different shades of skin colour passing us. While we were only used to seeing people who were mainly light-skinned, we were mesmerized by many natives with golden and olive-skinned descendants of Italians, Turks, Greeks, and even Jews.

We noticed people entering Hotel America's impressive glass façade and debated for a moment as to whether we should enter. Reluctantly, Papa pushed the revolving door and we walked into the hotel's glamorous lobby.

What a lobby!

My family was dazzled by the luxurious surroundings.

Palm trees growing inside the hotel. "Unreal," Papa whispered.

Large framed mirrors hung on the walls, leather sofas and armchairs were strategically positioned for maximum comfort. These were complemented by marble tables, both large and small, as well as Oriental and Turkish rugs on parquet floors.

"Magnificent," Mama breathed.

Huge crystal chandeliers glared at us, chiming softly in the sea breezes.

"Pretty," Misha giggled.

Crystal chandeliers did not impress me then, but something caught my eye, something far more intriguing than the décor. My favourite food: bagels.

Just a few feet inside the hotel, I read the word BAKERY. Looking closer, I could see shelves, packed with loaves of different sorts of bread – round, oval, square. Also, I noticed bagels with poppy seeds, and sesame seeds, while others with caraway seeds or plain. "Mama, look at that bakery. It's just like Kiev's."

No response.

I tried again, a little more insistent, "those bagels... I want one so bad... Can I? Please?" Papa dug out a couple of *liras* from his hidden wallet and we all walked to the bakery. Minutes later, everybody had a bagel. I started to dance with happiness.

We only had enough money to stay at this luxurious hotel for one or two nights, before we had to make proper arrangements for ourselves. When we checked in, we were astounded by the luxury of the room: the softness of the bed, and the silky fabric of the curtains. All of this was so foreign to us. All of us also stayed in a single room, magnificent compared to the crampiness of the train. Alek, Grandma Yael, Mama, Papa, Misha and myself slept so soundly that night. Even the floor of the carpet was luxurious.

The next day, Alek and my father were speaking and planning our next steps. Alek knew some members of the Jewish community in Rome, and he was on the phone with people he knew to get us an apartment. We had enough money for a few months' rent, but no more than that.

In the meantime, I walked with Mama and Misha out through the beautiful lobby and onto the street. We ate bagels again for breakfast, and I felt as though I were in a dream. We went to the beach and played in the sand. In a final act of extravagance, Mama decided to buy Misha and I *gelato* (ice cream). We had never had such a treat before.

The *gelato* I ate was chocolate flavoured, and it was the best thing I had ever tasted. Misha also took a lick and screamed, "Mmmmmm, yummy!" Mama laughed for the first time in as long as I could remember. She grabbed Misha and gave him a big hug.

We returned to our hotel and Alek was still on the phone, and Papa was still pacing the room. "I need to look for work," he told Mama. Mama sighed. "Please darling, let us just enjoy this time.

We will have plenty of time to worry later." Papa scoffed. "I can't afford to worry later about finding a job. I need to look now."

Grandma Yael did not look well at all; her skinned had yellowed considerably since we had arrived to Italy. She left the room and told us she would be back shortly.

She collapsed in the hotel lobby, trying to find the washroom. The concierge called the room. He was yelling in Italian, but we could not understand him. Papa, Mama and I went to the lobby to clear up the confusion, and we saw Grandma Yael being taken away in a stretcher. Papa insisted that he go with them in the ambulance, but the paramedics were resisting him. Eventually, he forced his way inside.

Mama and I sat in shock as we saw them drive off into the streets of Rome. Finding the hospital was a nightmare for Mama. We did not speak the language, and neither did Alek. Alek had to make yet another phone call to find us a translator. After many phone calls and many nervous hours, we located the hospital, and wrote the address down.

Mama, Misha, and I were about to call a taxi when Alek hung up the phone. "Just a minute!" He shouted. "We have to leave the hotel tomorrow and we cannot afford to stay here. I will arrange to get us another hotel next to the hospital, and move all our belongings there. So, stay where you are when you get to the hospital, and I will come find you, and tell you where I am."

Mama cried when she heard this. What would we do without our guardian angel, Alek? He saved us so many times, and all because of what my father did for him back in the camps. It was astounding that such a seemingly minor act of generosity paid off in spades years afterwards.

We took a taxi through the streets of Italy with Misha on my lap. The drivers in this country were just as crazy as back home, and we feared we would be involved in an automobile accident on the way to the hospital. We were dropped off at the wrong hospital and had to take another taxi to the correct one.

By the time we finally found my dear Grandma Yael, she had passed. Papa was beside himself. He was sobbing uncontrollably. Not only had he lost his father, but now he lost his mother, and his homeland too. He lost his job, his house, and his cottage. He had finally reached his breaking point, and there was no consoling my poor Papa. We just hugged him and waited for Alek to come and get us.

I remembered all the wonderful times I had with Grandma Yael. She was so kind and so loving. She was a woman whose pure joy in life was the smiles and laugher of others. I remembered when she read my fortune and made me laugh. She was a selfless woman. A truly selfless woman, and I never forgot her.

Late into the night we waited. I asked Papa if he wanted me to say any prayers for Grandma Yael, and he told me he did. I said the mourner's prayer and he hugged me tightly afterwards.

"I am immensely proud of you for learning the Jewish customs and prayers. You are a wonderful, kind, and good daughter. Grandma and grandpa were enormously proud of you, and you need to remember this," he told me. Misha was crying because he was so overtired. A beautiful Italian nurse gave him a lollipop and carried him to us and placed him on the floor by Mama.

"*Grazie*!" Mama checked her dictionary, and said in Italian. Finally, Alek arrived and told us he had found us another hotel near St. Peter's Basilica. This was a completely different area of the city with buildings of marble and gold pillars. Fountains with crystal clear water stood in front of these impressive structures, and even though I was exhausted, I was still aware enough to be struck by these magnificent structures.

Everyone slept in the hotel except for Papa. In the morning, he had dark rings around his eyes and could barely eat. He was depressed. We were all overwhelmed by this unfamiliar environment and by what had just happened. Alek made more and more phone calls until he eventually found a house in a neighbourhood with Jews who had also escaped the Soviets. The city Alek found was called Frascati.

Frascati was located outside of Rome on the Alban Hills close to the ancient city of Tusculum. We rented a small apartment with a wonderful view of the quiet street. Mama and Papa had one room, and Misha and I had another room, all to ourselves. Alek slept on the floor of the living room, because the apartment did not yet have adequate furniture.

His stay was only temporary anyway. Within a few days he managed to get himself his own apartment that was located a close drive away.

It took some time for us to settle down and adapt to our new environment, but eventually we did, and the spring turned into a gloriously hot and sunny summer. This was the summer I turned eleven years old, and Misha began to speak more.

On my birthday, my parents took me out for my favourite Italian treat. *Chocolate gelato*. We found a little place in town, and they gave me a big scoop for my birthday. Then Mama asked me if there was anything special I would like to do for the remainder of my special day.

I did not have to think twice. "The beach," I exclaimed. We did not have a car, so we all took a taxi to the beach and observed the relaxing sights and sounds of the ocean. It was marvellous to relax like that. Even Papa was able to relax a little. Misha built sandcastles and I took his hand and we swam in the ocean together for the first time. He got salt in his mouth and made a silly face. He was becoming a funny boy, and he liked to pretend and make jokes with me.

I remember my eleventh birthday so well because the atmosphere around it was so relaxed. Everyone seemed so happy and so blissful. It was the way a truly special day should be lived.

Shortly after my birthday, my parents had no choice but to come back to reality. They needed to learn the language and needed to find jobs. Mama began learning Italian after she put Misha to bed during the night, and Papa looked for any work in which he did not have to speak Italian. It was a challenging task to accomplish, but it was possible. The community of Jews was small, but always willing to help.

There was a small engineering firm run by a Russian Jewish man who operated out of a town not too far away. They were in need of a draftsman, and Papa went to interview for the position. We were on pins and needles as we awaited his return. If Papa did not secure this job, we would not be able to pay for rent for the next month.

Mama paced the apartment and practiced Italian out loud, trying to pretend as though everything were okay. I could tell she was nervous. To take her mind off the news, I suggested that we go to the bakery together to buy some bread. The Italians made the best bread and the best bagels. They made the best baguettes too. I was in love with the food from the very beginning.

A small bakery also run by a Jewish man named Haim and his wife Sheba was located about a block away from our apartment. It was a lovely place to live, because everything was so convenient, and the people were so nice and fashionable.

People here had money; they were far more relaxed when they had money. Even the hatred between the races were lessened with money. It was a far easier place to live than where we came from.

We walked into the bakery and Haim greeted us warmly. He wore a gold chain around his neck, and he had a hunched back from bending in front of the oven all day. "What can I get my two favourite ladies?" He asked us, jokingly.

"We will take a dozen bagels and a loaf of rye bread," Mama told Haim. "Sure thing," he said. His wife Sheba emerged from the back and addressed Mama before we could leave. "Does your little girl have a place to go to school?" She asked. Mama was taken aback. Her mind was on Papa's job and she could not answer, so I answered.

"I don't have a school to go to because I don't know Italian language," I told Sheba. Sheba snapped her finger. "Well, my daughter goes to Hebrew school. The classes start in two weeks. If you want, I can call the headmaster and arrange a meeting." Mama thanked Sheba profusely. It was a wonderful offer, and it was needed. School was not a priority on Mama and Papa's mind at this time. Italy was only supposed to be a temporary stop.

We still did not know for how long we would be in Italy, so to make plans for school seemed premature.

Still, while we waited, it was good to have options. I knew Mama would forget, so I wrote down the details and put it in my dress for later. When we arrived home, Papa was smiling. We knew he had good news for us, and I was absolutely correct.

Not only had he gotten the job, but the kind owner of the engineering firm offered twice the salary my father expected. We could afford the apartment now, but Mama wanted to be cautious. "If you lose your job or something happens, it's best we save everything we can," she said. Papa agreed.

Papa and Mama were very sensible when it came to these things. Now that Mama did not need to work, she devoted more time to learning Italian, and eventually she became fluent, but not during the time we were there. She continued her studies after we left Italy.

I really wanted to go to Hebrew school. The proposition by the baker's wife, Sheba, really excited me. For the time being, I made do with Grandpa Elie's books and enjoyed the seemingly endless sun of the Italian summer. My skin became quite tanned, and I loved how it felt. It felt good to be in the sun that long, but Mama would scold me if I spent too much time. It was apparently bad for your complexion.

The women who came from Eastern Europe were fair skinned. They liked to wear hats and veils to protect them from the sun. They were not like the native Italians with an olive complexion. The women like Mama and I would burn if we were out for too long. Even Misha and Papa would burn.

So, some days I did not go outside like Mama asked. I would stay at home and read. It was fascinating to read about our people, especially how the land of Rome fit into our history.

After Persia defeated the Babylonians, Jews returned to Palestine and the Temple was rebuilt. Then the Greeks defeated the Persians, and the Romans defeated the Greeks. Under the Romans, the Second Temple was destroyed in the year 70 C.E.

Despite the disruption, Jewish life continued under the rule of the Romans. There was a constant studying, and interpreting, and a reinterpreting of the Bible. Scholars did not always agree. The two rival schools of the first century, the disciples of Hillel and the disciples of Shammai, differed on so many of the points of Jewish law, even on such minor matters as whether the Hanukkah lights should be kindled from the right to the left, or from the left to the right. Of course, the Jews who lived in 1970s Rome had no preference one way or another.

What I found to be most interesting about Grandpa Elie's texts was the finding that Judaism was more than just a religion. It was a way of life. Over the centuries it created standards of practice, most of which have been put into law, and that this law was forever changing.

Years later I would reflect on such laws that I was only beginning to understand at this age. For instance, the laws around death and mourning. Grandpa Elie and Grandma Yael had completely different rituals around their death. Many of the laws that we could observe for Grandma Yael were not possible for Grandpa Elie. I thought about how G-d would view such events. In my younger years, I worried that he would be angry with me. As I got older, I realized that he certainly would not.

My heart was always in the right place. I always prayed for them and I always tried to do the right thing. The Soviets prohibited the observance of our sacred laws for grandpa Elie, and the language barrier prevented the observance for Grandma Yael. There was nothing I could do, and I thought G-d would forgive me as long as my heart was in the right place.

Living in Italy also made it difficult to follow the dietary laws. The Italians were famous for mixing meat and milk. Lasagna and pizza are an excellent example. They would serve lasagna with meat and cheese. I longed to observe the dietary laws of our religion, and for the first time ever, we began keeping a truly kosher kitchen. This was so wonderful to me.

Papa came home one day tired from work and I asked him about Hebrew school. I wanted to go to Hebrew school, and I told him about what the baker's wife Sheba told Mama. He exhaled and rubbed his forehead. He was not in the mood to discuss such things, but I was persistent.

"Papa, I really want to go to Hebrew school. Please let me go, please." Papa paced around the room. He was trying to avoid me. "Darling, please, I don't know for how long we will be in this country. I also don't know how expensive it is. We need to think about our next steps."

This answer did not satisfy me. I was extremely disappointed, but I did not say anything. Instead, the next day I ran to the bakery and asked Sheba if she knew how much Hebrew school would cost. "Well, I think that is a matter your parents should discuss with the headmaster," she told me. "Very well, can you give me the name and address of the headmaster?" At first Sheba was reluctant to give me this information, but even at the age of eleven, I was very persuasive, and she abide.

"Why would you give her that information, and not her parents?" Haim asked, as I left the store. "I trust her," said Sheba. "I have a good feeling about that little girl. She is a determined little one." Haim snorted. "She's a child! Her parents need to handle such matters."

The headmaster's house was on a hill closer to the center of the city. I remember the picket fence outside his home, and he was wearing a *kippah*. He was a religious man. I wondered why Papa never wore one. I wish he would have now that he was free to do so.

The headmaster's name was Mr. Abramowitz, and I walked up the hill and waved at him. Headmaster Abramowitz was a short bald man who wore a *Sephardic kippah* of many different colours. He paused when he saw me in the garden and greeted me warmly. "Hello little girl, can I help you?" he asked me.

"Yes, sir." I said. "I very much want to attend the Jewish school. I do not know if my parents can afford it, but my grandmother gave me money for my education, and I would like to give all of it to you, if you will admit me."

The headmaster laughed when I produced the tin my grandmother gave me with Russian currency. Headmaster Abramowitz had not seen those in quite some time. He looked very much like a Hungarian Jew.

"Please put your *kopeks* away," he said very warmly. "I will see if I can talk with your parents and work out a deal."

I walked back to our little apartment and felt a sense of relief. I thought I might finally have a Jewish education. I was also relieved at the absence of waiting in lines in order to enter the stores in this country. There were hardly any lines for anything.

Women wore wonderful fabrics of brown and orange, and I frequented the fashion district just to look at them in awe. When I finally arrived at the apartment, Alek was again with my father. Mama had adapted to the cuisine of the new country, and had made us all a plate of pasta.

It was incredibly good, and sweet. Alek spoke frankly with my father, as he always had. "The time has come to decide where we will go. I have terrible news that you might not want to hear, but I am going to tell you. We cannot go to Israel. There simply are not enough visas available at this time. We can stay here in Italy, or we can leave for a new land with a larger Jewish community, and perhaps even more opportunities," said Alek.

Papa looked concerned. "I think this country has been good to us, Alek. I have a job. The salary is good. Everyone seems happy here." Alek nodded and he tasted the pasta for the first time. He complemented Mama's cooking. Indeed, it was a good pasta.

"Yes, this is true," said Alek. "This is indeed true, however here you will not be able to afford a car. You will not be able to move from this apartment. The opportunity is limited, and citizenship here is extremely hard to come by."

"There is no guarantee you can become a citizen, and if you overstay your visa, they could send you back. The more realistic option is Canada or the United States. There, with a skill like you have, citizenship is almost guaranteed, and the opportunities are immense. Not to mention, a tremendous Jewish community there. They are not communists, they are capitalists, and they do not hate the Jews. It is not in their history. To move there would be to start completely new. A new life full of promise," said Alek.

"That's right," added Mama. "The Italians tolerate us, but they don't like us. Sheba has told me stories of America. She says they are far more tolerant there."

Papa thought and thought. He hardly touched his pasta. This was a big decision, and he had to think about it. We thanked Alek and he left. Alek did not have the money for a car in Italy. He walked back to his small apartment.

"What about Israel?" I asked Papa. "Why can't we go to Israel?" The answer was that there were too many applications to go to Israel. Canada and the United States were the realistic options for us.

We did not make the decision right away. Mama and Papa talked and talked. I was anxious during this time do discover what their verdict was.

In the meantime, I made friends with Sheba's daughter, Ruth. Ruth was exactly my age and she wore large framed glasses as was the style at the time. She had wonderful magazines from the United States that her parents bought for her. Fashion magazines.

We were both interested in fashion and cars. The cars in Italy were beautifully designed. My favourite car was the Ferrari, but this was a different time. Little girls were not supposed to like cars. They were supposed to like fashion, so Ruth and I spoke mostly about dresses and fashion designers.

I also asked Ruth about what it was like at the Jewish school. She complained about the teachers and about the homework, but I told her. "You should be thankful that you even get to attend. I pray that I will be able to attend one day. Back home they spat on you if they found out you were Jewish."

Ruth was taken aback by how forceful I was. "Well, the Italians don't like Jews either," she told me. "You don't understand the difference between the Italians and the Soviets," I said loudly. "You can't understand."

I frightened Ruth and we got into a little argument. She could not have understood what I went through, and it saddened me. Still, I understood that I should not have been so forceful. When Sheba and Haim came to see what the matter was, I apologized to my friend Ruth, and she accepted.

I wondered how long this friendship would last, and I became nervous that I would lose Ruth too. All the friendships that came and went had a profound effect on me as a child. I did not feel as close to Ruth, and so we fought occasionally. I missed my friend Marta. I desperately wanted to try to write her again, but I knew better than that.

I had already been warned once by Mama, and I would not defy her. I made sure to respect Mama just like I respected Papa. All my learning over the years about Judaism was done on my own. I never had the time or the money to attend the Hebrew school. I also never had a *bat-mitzvah*.

This was the one aspect of the religion that bothered me, but I grew to adapt and apply my own interpretation to behave in a way that lessened the patriarchy of the religion. Society in biblical times was patriarchal. The function of woman, it was thought, was to serve the man. When a woman married, she became the property of her husband. In fact, the original word for marriage was kinyan, an acquisition.

Even the bible states clearly that woman was created to be a helpmate to her husband. The status of Jewish women improved in post-biblical and Talmudic times, especially compared with the lot of women in society at large. Still, the Jewish woman was far from equal in relation to the Jewish man.

Nevertheless, women were still respected and were not abused. This was certainly true in my family. My father never hit or abused my mother, and I was thankful for this. What I found astounding, was that it was only in 1972, just a few years before our arrival in Italy, that a Reform seminary, the Hebrew Union College-Jewish Institute of Religion, ordained a woman as a rabbi.

This was indeed a historical event that hardly anybody knew about, but I knew about it, and Mama knew about it. Today, Jewish feminists, many of whom are Orthodox, have become vocal protagonists for change in Jewish law, so that women may share with men the privileges and obligations of Jewish living. The manner in which the desired changes should be accomplished is constantly grappled with by all branches of Judaism.

I would later consider myself to be a true feminist, although I was never Orthodox. I developed an extraordinary interest in the difference between laws and tradition. There are many Jewish rituals that women do not practice, even though they are legally permitted to do so. For example, even though Jewish law in theory allows a woman to act as a ritual slaughterer (*shochet*), this is traditionally a male occupation, and women are discouraged from entering it.

The same is true of circumcision. Jewish law permits a Jewish woman to act as a *mohel*. Although tradition does not consider it a proper female occupation, because it might offend the public's sensibility. This attitude prevails, even though early in the bible, Tzipora, the wife of Moses, circumcised her son.

My great yearning for justice, coupled with my introduction to the Jewish texts by Grandpa Elie, motivated me to learn about my religion and identity in depth. Over the years, I would develop my understanding, but these key, early years, significantly influenced the course of my life.

Chapter Fourteen

The Final Destination

THE FINAL TIME ALEK AND my father spoke together in our apartment was perhaps one of the most important meetings. Alek had some big news for us all, and he brought us some *gelato* to eat as a treat.

I was happy because I was given my favourite flavour, chocolate. He addressed Mama, Papa and me. Misha was still too young to realize what was going on. "I have made the decision for myself. I am going to New York City, and I am going to the American embassy tomorrow to apply. Will you come with me?" he asked Papa.

Mama and Papa had to think about it, but they had already been thinking for weeks. It was finally time to make the decision. "Yes," said Papa. "We will go to New York City too."

I was disappointed we were not going to Israel, but excited that we were going to America. Mama lamented, "Why did I spend all this time studying Italian then?" But in truth, Mama liked enjoyed studying Italian, and she would continue to study.

We were all excited at the prospect of going to America. At this point we had been in the country for four months, and because we knew it was only a temporary stop, we were anxious to move on to our final destination.

Mama began reading Italian books, and instead of studying Judaism, I learned from her. Mama read a fascinating book called The Prince, by Machiavelli.

When I would read it later as a young woman, I thought of how ironic it was, reading Machiavelli in Italy, after escaping the Soviets. I never would have dreamed that in the year 2020, the politics of the United States would begin to resemble the sinister themes espoused by that small, but extraordinarily significant book.

Papa and Alek spent the entire day at the American embassy. They waited in line and filled out all the required paperwork. A week passed before we received the disturbing news that Alek was approved for a visa, while Papa, Mama, Misha, and I were not.

It was a shock, but we were happy for Alek. It was truly a bittersweet moment in that little Italian apartment.

Of course, this news did not dissuade Alek from doing everything in his power to help us. His contacts were in the small Jewish community in Rome. They were not at the American embassy. Even though I thought Alek could do anything, his influence was limited in this situation. If the Americans would not take us, then we had no choice but to apply to Canada.

Papa wasted no time in such matters. We located the Canadian embassy the next day, and Papa took off from work to apply. If Canada would say no, then we were really stuck. Luckily, we got the good news couple of months later in the mail.

We were all approved to move to Canada!

In total, we would need to spend seven months in Rome to wait for the all the paperwork to be finalized. It was an arduous process, but it determined the rest of my life.

Seven months was a long time for a little girl of eleven. Ruth became my best friend, and I did not end up going to the Hebrew school, or to any school. I learned from Mama and from the books left to me by my Grandpa Elie.

The final few weeks were perhaps the most memorable of my time spent in Rome. I was totally free to explore and enjoy everything the city had to offer. Back then I felt as though I could do anything, and I was completely free.

I wanted to learn how to ride a bicycle, and so Papa bought me a used bike and taught me on the little street in front of our apartment. After a few hours of practice, I was able to ride on my own, and I was off, exploring the streets of Rome. My friend Ruth learned how to ride a bicycle too, and we would ride together. We loved going to the beach, like little girls do.

I asked Ruth if she thought she would move to Israel one day. "I don't know," she told me. "I hope I do," she said. We watched little boys make castles in the sand, and I was reminded of my baby brother Misha.

"We were supposed to go to Israel," I told Ruth. "We were supposed to go to Israel and then the United States, but now we are going to Canada."

I did not have the words to express what I was feeling at the time, but now I think I felt perplexed. I thought it did not matter how many plans you made, or how hard you tried, eventually there came a point in which all your effort and all your planning would be in G-d's hands. Still, I thought it was important to try. I always fought for what I thought was right.

I had a lot on my mind during this time. I knew that we were approaching the last leg of the journey. What would Canada be like? All I knew was that it was very cold, and I did not want to go back to the cold. I liked feeling the warm sunshine on my face.

Ruth snapped her fingers and smiled. "Ah, I do know something about Canada," she told me. "They are ruled by the Queen of England. Canadian dollars have the face of the Queen on them. I know that," she told me.

Shortly before we left, I finished reading the remainder of Grandpa Elie's book. I finished learning about the Romans and the Jews. After the Roman occupation of Palestine in the first century C.E., the need for the establishment of amity between Jews and non-Jews became pronounced. Many laws and practices were introduced to help achieve it. In the Talmud, these laws and practices were explained as *mipnay darkay shalom* which means "for the sake of peace," or maintaining goodwill between the Jewish and non-Jewish communities.

Even back under the rule of the Soviets, we tried to get along. Rabbi Judah the Prince was the first scholar to think about this policy of harmony. He set the tone for future leaders by carrying on a dialogue with the Roman rulers, and owing to his political brilliance, he succeeded in maintaining goodwill and peaceful relations between the Jews and the Roman occupiers.

I found it so fascinating to learn about the history of Rome, while I still had the chance to see it myself. I found it astonishing that the Talmud states "we feed the poor of non-Jews, we comfort their mourners, and we bury their dead with the Jewish dead for the sake of peace."

We were such a peaceful people, and we desired nothing but a positive relationship with the non-Jewish people in the Soviet Union as well as Rome. It was in our history, yet most people were ignorant to this history. They simply saw our success and hated us because of it.

I read through the entire history of Rome and I discovered that even though Jews have tried to live in harmony with the larger Christian world, this has not always been easy or even possible to achieve.

On the one hand, the non-Jewish majority has not always been willing to allow Jews to enter its social circles, and display their brilliance in positions of prestige or power.

Papa, for example could never hope to be more than a draftsman in the Soviet Union, even though he was capable of so much more. Mama would never be promoted or even paid the same wage as a non-Jew who did the same work.

On the other hand, the Jewish people have not always been eager to have unnecessary contact with the non-Jewish community, out of fear that this may lead to assimilation. We had to stick together, but this was also an important part of survival. The issue was quite complex.

Rome has many crucifixes and images of Jesus. I developed an interest in Christianity, and I began reading more in depth about Jesus. Once, while walking in Rome, I heard someone refer to Jews as "Christ killers" and this sparked my interest. I began to read about Jesus in Rome, and discovered that Pontius Pilate, the Roman governor of Palestine in the time of Jesus, is portrayed in the New Testament as a leader without control over events.

The book of Matthew describes Pilate as accusing Jesus of being the King of the Jews, and hence a threat to Roman authority, and sentenced him to execution. The blame for the crucifixion was placed on the chief priests and the elders who said, "this blood is not shed by my hands," while the Jews responded that, "Jesus's blood be upon us and our children."

Here Matthew shifted the guilt for the crucifixion from the Romans to the Jews, and therefore the slur continues to be a problem for Jewish people to this day.

Over the seven months that we stayed in the apartment, we did not accumulate many material possessions. We had to decide again what was important to keep, and what we had to leave behind.

Papa ended up selling my bicycle, which I was quite upset about.

Alek left before us to America. We were in tears when we said goodbye to him. He hugged Papa for a very long time. "My good friend, where would I be without you," he told my father. My father shook his head.

"No, my friend, where would I be without you? You have done so much for me, and for our family. How can I ever repay you?"

Alek looked at my father with his beautiful eyes and smiled. "You can visit me in New York when you have the money. I do not want this to be the end. We must keep in touch," he said. Papa was very emotional, but he did not cry. He just nodded.

Alek then turned his gaze towards me and smiled once more. "Well Rebecca, I enjoyed working with you. Keep studying and be a good little girl, alright?"

"Yes, Alek," I said. I gave him a hug too. It was sad to see Alek leave for America. He was more than a friend. He was part of our family. It never got any easier, saying goodbye to all we grew accustomed to like.

I walked around the streets to watch the sunset, but I promised Mama and Papa that I would be back before it was dark outside. They had become more anxious, like I was, before our big move. I could not sit still, so I walked and walked. As I walked, I thought about what the journey had taught me thus far.

I thought about my sister, and I had a terrible feeling in the pit of my stomach. I needed to find some way to contact her, and make sure she was all right. I knew that when I would arrive to Canada I would. Thankfully, years later, after the Soviet Union ceased to exist, she left her husband, and went to live in Israel with a Jewish husband.

I also thought about all the friends I had made and lost along the way. I wondered where they were, and what they were doing. Would Canada bring new friends? Or would these people be as cold as the weather? These were the thoughts that were going through my mind as I walked the streets of Rome.

After I had walked off all my fears for the next leg of the journey, I was able to relax and take in my surroundings. Beautiful people zoomed around on these little motorcycles called *vespa*, and they looked so free. Soon I would be free to be who I was, and to live without fear.

Mama was finally able to shop without being beaten or ridiculed. Her Italian was coming along, and she even started a little garden on the balcony with tomato plants, basil plants, and flowers.

I had time to be a little girl again. I did not have to grocery shop for the family or help as much with chores. When Papa quit his job shortly before we departed, he was the happiest I had seen him in quite some time. He finally looked somewhat relaxed.

Leaving Italy was not quite like leaving the Soviet Union. We had not been there for long enough to make lasting friendships, but I did have Ruth, and Mama had Sheba.

A couple of days before we left, Mama picked all of the tomatoes and all of the basil, along with the flowers as well. I remember she grew beautiful orange flowers that resembled lilies, except they were not lilies. They were an orange and brown, and I called them Yael flowers, because they reminded me of my grandmother.

Mama and I walked to Sheba and Haim's bakery and gave them almost everything we had from our garden. "You were so kind to us," said Mama. "Please, this is the least we can do." Sheba and Haim were incredibly pleased and thankful. They felt bad not reciprocating, so they gave us a dozen bagels, and I suggested that we take everything back to the apartment for a party, like we did before we left home for the first time.

"That's a wonderful idea," said Haim. "She's a smart girl."

"See!" said Sheba. "I told you she was smart little girl." Sheba nudged me playfully, and Ruth joined us too.

We said goodbye to all our friends.

When it came time for us to leave for the airport, I was anxious again. All the anxiety came back to me. We sat in the airport and I looked at all the people in the terminal. Pilots with large, dark aviator sunglasses walked with glamorous flight attendants. Businessmen in fine Italian suits sipped whiskey and smoked cigars. The airport had an air of luxury to it. Flying was an event, except this was not a vacation for us. This was the plane ride to the rest of our lives.

Mama was just knowledgeable enough in Italian to order us food, and Papa was extremely impressed. "If you would have told me my wife would be speaking Italian this time last year, I wouldn't have believed it," he said, laughing.

Misha was fussy, so I asked Papa to buy him something from the gift shop to calm him down, and Papa bought us giant, multi-coloured lollipops. It was quite delicious, and our mouths turned red and blue from the food colouring.

Soon enough, it was time for our flight. In the lineup, there were businessmen and families. There were Italian soldiers, and the sight of them gave me a chill. I was reminded of the militia on the train and the KGB from back home.

It would take me a while before I became comfortable with seeing police officers or the military on the street. We were afraid of them, back in the Soviet Union. In Canada, they were our protectors. There would be many things I would come to learn about my new country.

I insisted on sitting near the window. As we boarded the plane, I remember how anxious I was to cross the Atlantic and start a new life in Canada. The stewardess gave us little napkins with maple leaves on them. We were on an Air Canada flight, and everyone seemed so friendly. They served us tomato juice, which I thought was strange, but it tasted good, but salty.

Though I was only eleven years old, I already knew that my children would now be born without fear and oppression. I smiled up at Mama. She smiled back at me. We were all happy and not afraid anymore. We felt as though we were on our way to a better life, where we would be free to be who we truly were.

Epilogue

Rebecca's Journey is a story about identity. Being a Jew under Soviet rule is completely different than being Jewish in a free and open society.

The key difference is blatant discrimination, and a pressure to abandon what it means to be Jewish. One's conviction and courage can only be truly tested and displayed during these trying times.

This is because pressure is placed upon the Jewish people to hide who they really are, and the alternative is so seemingly easy. "Just say that you are not Jewish."

Some are strong, while others cave to the pressure. If holding on to a Jewish identity is important, then suffering is inevitable. The suffering Rebecca experienced was tragically a reality of the time she lived through. However, this suffering was not in vain. It only served to strengthen her resolve to pass on Jewish values, and a Jewish identity to the next generation in a new land.

A Jewish person, under these unfortunate circumstances, must constantly question who they are and what is important to them.

When parents read Rebecca's Journey in the United States or in Canada, they might want to reflect on how lucky they are that their children have been brought up in the west.

They never had to go through what Rebecca went through. They were never truly tested as Rebecca and her parents were.

The cruelty Rebecca experienced is an enlightening tale for the current generation of American and Canadian Jews to read. It is a candid illustration of discrimination and true hatred towards Jews. In the end, because of her resilient nature, the support of her family, and her faith and conviction in who she was as a Jewish girl, she ended up making a life for herself. She could now openly express who she was and what she valued.

The historical context in which this novel takes place is important to study. It is important to know the history of the Jewish people. Between 1964 and 1974 there are many accounts of antisemitic activity that occurred in Russia and in the Ukraine.

The persecution of Jews during this time was horrific and perhaps even understated.

Jewish people could not practice their religion in the open. They were forced to hide like Rebecca and her grandparents. Today, people might think that life in Russia and the Ukraine has improved for Jewish people, but there is still a lot of antisemitism which is present.

Rebecca lived through what is now known as the "era of stagnation." It began in 1964 and ended in 1982. Fortunately for Rebecca, she and her family left before the economy disintegrated further. Just like the modern era, there is a strong correlation between economic hardship and antisemitic sentiment.

Brezhnev never used the term "era of stagnation" to define the period in which he led. He used the term "developed socialism." This period started in 1971. It is the period in which Rebeca became aware of her surroundings, and that of the population's true feelings towards Brezhnev.

The reality of life for the average person versus what was espoused on state television and radio were completely separate accounts.

Scholars of this period of history have disagreed on the dates and causes of the economic stagnation under Brezhnev. Supporters of Gorbachev have criticized Brezhnev and his policies, however other scholars point to a more nuanced explanation, citing industrial growth rates and the arms industry, which may or may not have changed under different leadership.

Most scholars also believe that economic stagnation began in 1975. ***Rebecca's Journey*** claims that this economic stagnation started far earlier, beginning in the 1960s. Indeed, determining the starting point of economic stagnation is much dependent on the demographic in question. Jews and other oppressed minorities, for example, were affected differently than the general population.

The Jewish community living under the Soviets at this time recognized the importance of leaving an increasingly dangerous situation.

They mobilized, with help from the American and Canadian Jewish community to leave, either to the west or to Israel.

After Brezhnev died in 1982, Yuri Andropov succeeded him as the Soviet leader. Modest reforms were introduced, and he died shortly after taking power. Konstantin Chernenko, the leader after Andropov, continued the work of his successor.

Quasi-capitalism and democratic reforms continued, but ultimately failed, leading to the dissolution of the Soviet Union in 1991.

The Jewish population could never thrive in an environment like the Soviet Union, but they were inordinately successful in Canada and the United States.

Rebecca moved to Montreal, Quebec, the second largest city in Canada. In 1970, the population of the Jewish community was approximately 121,000. Rebecca arrived in the mid-1970s, but the history of Jews in Montreal dates back to 1760.

Merchants, fur traders, exporters, and importers were amongst the first Jewish people to settle in Montreal, and they moved there from New York, where Alek would eventually settle.

When Rebecca arrived with her parents in Montreal, there were about forty synagogues. Thirty-three were Orthodox, three were Conservative, three were Reform, and one was Reconstructionist. There were opportunities in Montreal that were far better than in the Soviet Union. Rebecca's family did not get to stay long in Montreal, and soon after the Canadian government moved Rebecca and her family to Edmonton, Alberta in order to balance Jewish population across Canada.

As the Jewish population increased, it became self-supporting through industrious members like Alek. They fund-raised, multiplied, and gained influence. Shortly before Rebecca landed in Canada, in 1970, Victor Goldbloom was re-elected as a member of the Quebec provincial legislature. He became the first Jewish person to become a cabinet minister in the Quebec provincial government.

In more recent years, the Jewish population has been composed of several diverse groups that settled in Canada during different times, and under different circumstances.

Rebecca was amongst the most recent wave. Others included Jews from France, Argentina, and a small number of Ethiopian Jews from Israel.

An important lesson to take away from Rebecca's Journey is that the freedom to study the sacred Jewish texts is sacred. It is a continuous battle, fought by the Jewish people for thousands of years.

Without this battle, there can be no Jewish people, and no Jewish identity. The Jewish people must fight and win, or face extinction.

Rebecca teaches us that this battle cannot be won without the resolve and courage displayed by Jewish people. This story shows us the horror and darkness of hate and antisemitism, and offers a solution to it. The solution is a will to fight for an identity that is distinctly Jewish.

The tale can be compared to the biblical tale of David and Goliath, which has taken on the meaning of an underdog situation, in which the weaker opponent faces a much bigger and stronger adversary.

The fact that Rebecca is such a young girl is striking when one considers her inspiring courage to stand up to force as large and "goliath like" as antisemitism in the Soviet Union.

Another lesson to take away is the lesson of hope. Hope is a particularly important in Rebecca's Journey. Without hope, Rebecca and her parents would have given up and stayed. The fate for Jewish people who stayed longer than Rebecca was even more precarious. Remaining hopeful is perhaps one of the most important state of minds to continue the fight against antisemitism.

Facing an ugly hatred should not discourage a Jewish person from practicing their religion, and being open about who they are. It may scare them, and it may challenge them, but this hatred must never be "the cause" to abandon one's identity.

Throughout all her struggles, Rebecca never doubts that what she is fighting for is "justice." She is fighting against "injustice," which in her journey, is the antisemitic sentiment she experienced in the Soviet Union.

Antisemitism can be attributed to ignorance and blind hatred, but Rebecca's Journey prompts Jews in the Diaspora to reflect on the nature of antisemitism itself.

Why did she encounter such hatred? What is the reason for all this hatred? The reader of this book is well advised to study more history to expand their understanding of such phenomenon, just as Rebecca did.

It is conceivable that one of the many important reasons why Rebecca is so strong in her fight for justice also has to do with theological differences. There are key theological differences, from a historical perspective, that set Jewish people apart from other religions like Christianity.

It is particularly interesting to consider these theological differences when reflecting on emerging antisemitism in our current political environment. Take for example the concept of "original sin." St. Augustine was the first theologian to teach that man is born into this world in a state of sin. The basis of this belief is the Bible.

Rebecca never feels this way. The doctrine of original sin is totally unacceptable to Jews. Jews believe that man enters the world free of sin, with a soul that is pure and innocent and untainted. Rebecca's character is the embodiment of this Jewish soul who struggles to understand herself in an environment which persecutes her. She is pure, innocent, and untainted.

No matter how many incidents of violent antisemitism, Rebecca is able to overcome them. The reader might say that this is unrealistic, but if one considers a theological, perhaps even unconscious difference between her and her environment, this may provide the reader with an interesting explanation.

Perhaps a final lesson Rebecca's Journey illustrates is the importance of gratitude. Jews who appreciate the freedom to practice their religion, and show who they really are, must be grateful for what they have, because the freedoms Jewish people have worked so hard to obtain are precarious.

The state of the world continues to change, and Jews in the Diaspora must be grateful for their freedoms, but also vigilant. They must watch for the same political and ideological warning signs that Rebecca experienced.

Rebecca knew who she was, and what she was fighting for: a Jewish identity, and a freedom to be Jewish and to live in peace. The next generation must take the lessons from her and others like her, to truly understand the courage and tenacity it takes to fight for what you believe in, and to never give into antisemitism.

www.ingramcontent.com/pod-product-compliance
Lightning Source LLC
Chambersburg PA
CBHW070956180726
48291CB00004B/1319

* 9 7 8 1 9 2 7 5 3 8 8 3 8 *